SEPARATE HOUSES

A handbook for divorced parents

Robert B. Shapiro, *Ph.D., is an experienced family counselor and director of Clinical Psychology Associates in Chicago, Illinois. During his 15 years in private practice, Dr. Shapiro has specialized in working with families and relationship problems. He has worked closely with judges and attorneys and has conducted custody evaluations throughout his professional career. He was a founding psychologist of the DuPage County (Illinois) Conciliation/Mediation Program in 1986 and remains an active member. Dr. Shapiro is a frequent lecturer on divorce and custody issues.*

SEPARATE HOUSES

A handbook for divorced parents

Robert B. Shapiro, Ph.D.

Bookmakers Guild, Inc.

Lakewood, Colorado

Published in 1989 in the United States of America by
Bookmakers Guild, Inc.
9655 West Colfax Avenue
Lakewood, Colorado 80215

Printed and bound in the United States of America

Hardcover: ISBN 0-917665-36-8
Paper: ISBN 0-917665-37-6

Library of Congress Cataloging-in-Publication Data

Shapiro, Robert B., 1944–
  Separate houses : a handbook for divorced parents / by Robert B. Shapiro.
p.   cm.
ISBN 0-917665-36-8 : $12.95—ISBN 0-917665-37-6 (pbk.) : $7.95
1. Custody of children—United States—Popular works.
2. Visitation rights (Domestic relations)—United States—Popular
works. I. Title.
KF547.Z9S46   1989
346.7301'7—dc20
[347.30617]   89-14992
                                                                            CIP

dedicated to
LOUIS B. SHAPIRO, M.D.,
my dad

Other Child Advocacy Titles from Bookmakers

Shall the Circle Be Unbroken?
   Helping the Emotionally Maltreated Child
   by Marilyn Holm

Foundations of Child Advocacy
   Edited by Donald C. Bross and Laura Freeman Michaels

Malpractice and Liability in Child Protective Services
   Edited by Wayne Holder and Kathleen Hayes

Contents

5. CONCLUSIONS AND TESTS,   79

Acknowledgments

"Thank you," like "I'm sorry" and "I love you," tends to be an overused sentiment in our society, and in its overuse loses meaning. Yet it becomes increasingly clear that few, if any of us, accomplish very much without the influence, support, and help of others. The following people, each in their own way, influenced my writing and had a major impact on this book. I am extremely grateful to these people, and consequently *these* "thank yous" are heartfelt and sincere.

I continue to be amazed at all that is involved in bringing a book through its entire publication process. I am deeply grateful to Barbara J. Ciletti, my publisher, for her interest and belief in my ideas, and for her professionalism throughout all phases of the process that have brought this book to print.

No amount of thanks can adequately convey my appreciation to my wife Dayle. She has supported my writing from the very beginning. She has helped to keep me focused, and has contributed many ideas to this book. But perhaps her most important contribution is what she has taught me about being a parent. Her willingness to give of herself and her acceptance and love for all the children in our blended family are examples of unselfishness that have influenced my writing, affected my parenting, and will long be remembered by our children.

My deep appreciation goes out to our children Rachel, Tracy, Ross, Roni, and Cameron. The pain and sorrow they have experienced and the adjustments they have made through adolescence, divorce, remarriage, and the blending of families have been the inspiration for this book. Their determination to succeed and grow has greatly enhanced my motivation to write. Their happiness has added to my joy. Indeed, they are very special people.

The honorable Judges Robert A. Cox and Michael Galasso have been instrumental in the development and implementation of the highly successful conciliation/mediation program in DuPage County, Illinois. Without this program many couples and their children would have been subjected to bitter, traumatic, lengthy, and expensive court battles over issues of custody and visitation. On behalf of these families, I am grateful to both these men, their judicial colleagues, and the handful of psychologists who have participated in making this program successful.

It has been a joy and a privilege to be the director and staff member of Clinical Psychology Associates. This is a group of highly dedicated professionals who enjoy their work and whose support and friendship have had a lasting effect on me. I am especially appreciative of the contributions made by Ms. Sheila Jacobson, who not only helps run our offices and puts up with the varying moods of patients and staff alike, but who also found time to type, correct and retype this manuscript. Her dedication to this job, her loyalty to me, and the caretaking role she plays in the office are often taken for granted, but never forgotten.

While the material in this book has drawn from my twenty or so years as a clinical psychologist, and in particular my years of doing custody evaluations and conciliation/mediation work, its inspiration largely stems from my own childhood experiences as well as my children's pain and growth. I am exceptionally fortunate to have grown up in a family filled with love and time for me. My parents have been married fifty-eight years, and much of their life has been dedicated to helping others. My mother's gentleness and caring ways have greatly influenced me, and you will see this reflected in both my writing and my beliefs about parenting. My father has been a parent, a teacher, and a friend to me for all my years. His intolerance of self-deception and his quest for truth have been a guiding beacon throughout my life. His passion for reading and his appreciation for the power and influence of written ideas have clearly become a part of me. I will forever fondly remember hours we spent together reading when I was a boy. It is for these reasons and so many more that I dedicate this book to him.

Foreword

As the presiding judge of the Domestic Relations Court of DuPage County (the largest county in the state of Illinois except for Cook County), I have witnessed the devastating effects of divorce on the family unit. The judicial system can strive for sensitivity and compassion in an attempt to minimize the trauma to the nuclear family, but universally, by the nature of the system itself, it has severe limitations.

The judicial system inherently is both confrontational and adversarial. Through these processes it seeks to elicit the truth. That truth-seeking process in family matters creates a tension that in some instances has no limits. One must not forget that the court system seeks to develop legal and logical solutions for people who, because of the tension, cannot be logical. As a result there are many instances wherein the implementation of the court orders is resisted by the parties, thus creating more confrontation and tension. The nuclear family cannot be isolated from the tension and trauma of a divorce unless alternative methods of dealing with family issues are available to the court system.

Most states have recognized the legal dilemma and have enacted statutes of authorized alternative methods to deal with the divorce crisis. Court-ordered mediation, conciliation and/or counseling are becoming quite commonplace. The jury is still out as to which programs are the most effective. However, there is no dispute that regardless of the program our children have benefited. The mindset is slowly being transformed from what the parents need and want to what is in the best interest of the child.

Any program that has developed a track record of success has at its core a component which allows the child's needs and interests to be expressed and protected. The latter can only be accomplished by educating and informing the parents.

Separate Houses is a book that does just that. It takes parents through a step-by-step process which will help them understand their problems, the needs of their children, and the limitations of the judicial system.

Michael R. Galasso
Presiding Judge, Domestic Relations Division
Circuit Court of the 18th Judicial Circuit
DuPage County, Illinois

Introduction

This book is intended to be an easy-to-read guide for parents going through divorce or otherwise struggling with issues pertaining to visitation and custody. It has been written with the best interests of the children in mind, to help you understand the psychological needs of your children in response to a divorce, but without the usual psychological jargon. *Separate Houses* is meant to be a reference book: something to be read once, then referred back to as the issues come up. There is a great deal going on in your life right now. Worries about the children; where and how you and they will live; issues of security, employment, and money; and the reactions of family and friends all dominate. You don't need or want to labor through a 500-page treatise about custody and divorce. Furthermore, you don't want to read about *all* the possible outcomes of *all* the possible situations.

With that in mind, this book has been written directly and to the point. Herein are basic things to do and certain things not to do. In most cases there are simple reasons for them. These reasons will be addressed. Each subject will be dealt with in no more than two pages. The dos and don'ts can be looked at as rules to follow. However, as with all rules, there are exceptions. All the possible exceptions can't be covered in this book, again, because it is a handbook. In addition, most of the exceptions will require your seeking professional help for answers, not using self-help books. For example, a general rule you'll see later in this book is that women should have custody of infants and very young children (see "Custody of Infants and Preschoolers" in Chapter 2). However, if the mother is an active alcoholic or schizophrenic, other custodial arrangements should certainly be considered. This section of the book wouldn't apply, and a mental health professional should be consulted.

As painful as divorce is and as unique as it feels when you're living through the experience, most divorces follow simple formulas. Children's responses to divorce are fairly predictable, and therefore the rules are fairly straightforward and direct. I can't guarantee your children won't have any problems if you follow these rules, but I can state with confidence that their problems will not stem solely from the divorce.

There are five chapters in this book. The first chapter deals with universal issues of custody and visitation regardless of the stage you're in. Chapters 2, 3, and 4 deal with different stages of the process; going through divorce, living with custody and visitation issues, and changing custody and visitation arrangements. The last chapter contains general summary information and two tests. The first test is one that may help you and your spouse determine which of you should have custody. The second test will help you determine how well you and your ex-spouse are responding to the needs of your children. At some point all five chapters may be applicable to you and your children.

Your divorce, certainly destructive and perhaps volcanic, is nevertheless not the end of life. Some will experience almost immediate relief as the pain of a difficult marriage comes to an end. For others the peace will take longer to achieve. For all it is the foundation of a new life, an opportunity for change. Take hold of this new life and make the best of it you can.

Chapter 1

General Issues
of Divorce and Custody

Divorce Does Not Have To Destroy Children's Lives

For most people the hardest part about getting divorced is seeing the pain of the children. For half these people that pain is compounded by their own: They are leaving their children with the other parent. Issues of custody and visitation produce very powerful emotions in divorcing parents, and these issues are more commonplace today than ever before. Once it was a foregone conclusion that women got custody of their children, but our society has significantly changed in the past two decades. The women's movement has not only liberated women from traditional stereotypes, but has also raised the possibility that men may have the ability to successfully, and perhaps with superiority, carry out roles and functions previously believed the sole domain of women. While the divorce rate the past ten years has been holding constant at about 48 percent, custody conflict has risen sharply. More men are seeking custody of their children, and more men than ever who don't get custody are staying actively involved, as visiting parents, in raising their children.

The benefit to the children can be tremendous. Having two loving parents in their lives to provide male and female role models, to convey values, and to teach them about relationships, love, caring, and responsibility, can be invaluable. It can salvage an otherwise permanently scarring event—divorce.

Too often, however, the increased options available to parents today help create a battleground for couples to continue their marital war, using the children as heavy artillery. Sole custody, joint custody, residential custody with joint custody, and various levels of visitation are some of the options available. Picking the right combination of custody and visitation is the most important task of divorcing couples and should be attended to before any other decisions (e.g., those about property, money, etc.) are made. Divorce will clearly change the children's lives, but it will not destroy them if it is carried out with self-awareness and sensitivity to their needs. The passage of children through this period should be kept as stable and anxiety-free as possible. If it is a time of battle in which the self-serving needs and self-righteousness of adults take over, then the children will surely be deeply scarred.

Should We Stay Together or Separate Before the Divorce?

The general rule says to separate. For most couples the period leading up to divorce is very volatile. Once the children have been told about the divorce and had a chance to deal with what it will mean to them (see the next section, "How and What To Tell the Children and How They'll React"), the best solution to the volatility is to separate the adults. Even if custody is not at question in the divorce and there is a calming of the tension once the decision has been made to get divorced, separation is still a good idea.

There are a couple of reasons for this. As the negotiations begin on who gets what, more likely than not tempers will heat up again, and the anger and resentment in the marriage may get focused on and played out in "the settlement." Having the children witness the kind of anger that is often expressed during this period on top of dealing with the trauma of the divorce is simply too painful and should be avoided.

Furthermore, for young children, under the age of ten, it's terribly confusing, once they've been told about the divorce and what it will mean, to have mom and dad stay together. With one parent out of the house, they may start to deal with the pain and psychologically move forward. When parents stay together, the children are enabled to deny reality. This only prolongs the inevitable and makes the eventual coping with the divorce more difficult.

This advice holds true even if there is a custody dispute (disagreement about which parent should eventually have custody). In most states, even if you leave home without the children it will not have any bearing on the final custody outcome. Obviously this needs to be confirmed in your county and state through your attorney. If your attorney does recommend your staying in the home and your spouse also refuses to leave, then an in-house separation is essential for the sake of the children and in order to maintain some calm. Such a separation means the adults sleep in separate rooms and maintain essentially separate lives (independent coming and going, meals, etc.) within the home.

The only time this rule does not apply is when it is a relatively calm and amicable divorce and the children are older (all of them over ten). This situation is fairly unusual; and even then, it is suggested that the wait for separation not be too long.

How long should both parents stay in the home after the children have been told? About a month, but not less than two weeks. This rule does not apply, of course, in any family situations where, if all family members continue to live together, the health and/or safety of some of its members will be jeopardized. Where there is violence, child abuse, or child molestation, immediate separation and the family members' safety become the first priority.

How and What To Tell the Children and How They'll React

Regardless of their age, children should be told in advance that there will be a divorce and what it will mean for them. Obviously a child of two will understand it differently than a twelve-year-old, but even that two-year-old needs to be told and prepared for the separation, lest he simply wake up one morning and find daddy gone.

Kids are pretty observant creatures. Especially school-age children (exposed to divorce through their peers) will be perceptive enough to realize that there are serious problems. Consequently, long before you and your spouse have decided to end the marriage, or to tell the children, if a decision has been made, the children may be asking you if you are going to get divorced. All of this is to demonstrate that children of all ages are alive and sensitive to the feelings of their parents, the quality of their parents' inter-action, and changes in that quality. It is unfair to them not to let them know what is going on and what will happen to them with enough lead time for them to comprehend it, ask questions about it, and adjust to it.

When you know that you are definitely getting divorced and have worked out some of the details, so you can answer the chil-dren's questions, tell them. Make sure your decision is final—or as final as possible. Of course couples planning divorce sometimes put their marriages back together. But remember it is a terrible injustice to tell your children of the divorce and prepare them for the pain only to change your mind two days later. If there is more than one child, tell them together, regardless of the difference in ages and ability to understand. The implication of secrecy if they are told separately is worse than the confusion that sometimes occurs because of the children's different levels of understanding.

There will be several things all children want to know, so be prepared. Some of these things are decidedly self-centered and tend to trouble some parents; it can seem to them as if the children don't care about the parents' pain—only their own needs. Re-member, their sense of family, sense of wholeness, even their sense of identity is jeopardized by a divorce. Consequently they cling to whatever they can. Will we have to move? Will I still be able to keep my furniture? Do I have to change schools? Will I still see my friends? Can I still take piano lessons? Will I still get my new bike? Will we still have as much food? Can I still have the new pair of jeans you promised? These are some of the more common questions both parents and children have told me were asked after the children were informed about the divorce.

Answer the questions as honestly as possible. Don't tell the children what you think they want to hear only to disappoint them at a later date. If you don't have an answer to a question, tell them that and discuss the various possibilities.

Whatever you do, don't minimize their concerns or be angry at their reactions. In all that you tell them, you need to communicate to them that the divorce is not their fault. Marriage is not a child's responsibility, and divorce is never a result of a child's behavior. Some couples do argue incessantly about their kids; however, their inability to agree is imbedded in themselves and their marriage and is not a fault of the child.

Children will react emotionally in a variety of different ways. To be sure, tears and depression are common, especially from prepuberty age (twelve) on down. Teenagers, less predictable anyway, seem to have a variety of reactions and are likely to have more than one. Again, tears are common; so is anger and rage, sometimes expressed as "How could you do this to me?" If you have told the children about a month prior to you and your spouse separating, then you have allowed them significant time to get used to the inevitable, ask questions they need answers to, talk about their feelings, and begin to adjust.

Preschool children may also have a variety of reactions. If they see older children crying and upset, they will model that behavior and be upset as well. If there are no older children to model, they may ask a few questions and then, in the days to come, act as if nothing has changed. There will be more of a reaction when the actual separation takes place—then they will understand what divorce means (to them).

Where marriages have been very stormy, for example, with violence or alcoholism, you may experience a sense of relief in your children.

If your children show no reaction, ask few if any questions, or simply withdraw, then it is advisable to get professional help. Your attorney should be able to refer you to a mental health professional who specializes in working with families struggling with divorce issues.

Older children, especially, may ask reasons why. I strongly recommend that answers to these questions stay along the lines of "Mom and dad don't love each other anymore," or "We fight too much and don't want to live with each other anymore," or "The marriage was a mistake," etc. Even when there was obvious abuse, as in the case of alcoholism, I would avoid blaming or name-calling. The reasons for this are important and they will be explained in Chapter 2 (see "Blame for the Divorce"). In all of the telling, reassure the children that despite what is happening with mom and dad, they are loved, their needs are important and are being considered, and that they will continue to be loved.

What Does Custody Mean?

Most people think getting custody of their children in the divorce settlement is like getting the stereo. It's yours! Nothing could be further from the truth. No one ever really has possession of their children—and if more parents realized this, they wouldn't battle so much over the nonexistent right of "ownership." They would be more able to focus on the best interest of the child and stop worrying about losing something they never had.

Our children are in our care for approximately the first eighteen years of their lives (and some middle eighteen years of ours). From the time they start to crawl we begin to lose them. We can shape their values, mold their personalities, and influence the kinds of people they become, but they do not belong to us. By the time they are eighteen, they will decide whose house to go to at Thanksgiving and Christmas—the courts won't decide, the attorneys won't decide, and the parents won't decide.

What custody means is that during the time the children are in your care, you're responsible for their physical and emotional well-being and for the development of their values, character, and sense of right and wrong. What visitation means is that during the time the children are in your care, you are responsible for their physical and emotional well-being and for the development of their values, character, and sense of right and wrong. The only difference is that one parent spends more time with these responsibilities than does the other. Too often parents with visitation rights feel they have lost something. However, if visitation is reasonably frequent, they soon realize that they are still among the central figures in their children's lives and that they can still enjoy all the wonderful adult experiences associated with raising children.

For many adults (unless they have infants or young preschoolers), issues of custody and visitation only last about a decade.

During this time, the children's needs themselves will produce numerous changes in the custodial/visitation arrangement. It is hoped that you and your ex-spouse will be able to work these changes out together with your children. The alternative is repeatedly going to court, a process that is painful, angry, expensive, and emotionally draining.

As your children grow they will become more involved with their peer group, afterschool activities, perhaps athletics and other pursuits. Eventually they will drive and have, in general, increased mobility. They will no longer be of an age to tuck in bed at night, nor will they be willing to sit still for games with mom or dad. Consequently regular visitation may take on a different look. Short visits for dinner or getting together after a high school event may be more appropriate and meaningful for the teenager than regular weekend visits. This is not to suggest that these visits stop, only that the older the child becomes, the more there is a need for flexibility.

Lest you believe the noncustodial parent is the only one to suffer, the custodial parent also loses contact with the teenage child. Adolescents who get involved in their peer group's activities, part-time jobs, etc., spend less and less time with their parents. As they mature and become more intimate with their friends, the relationship with both parents becomes more distant, and contact lessens. Adults must remember that lessening contact does not mean lessening love. Even when a parent is part of an intact family, an adolescent's independence can feel like loss. When you are divorced and your adolescent has become independent and "on the go," seldom standing still for you, an announcement of dinner plans with the other parent can easily be experienced as rejection. At any age, the child's interest in the other parent is a real test of the custodial parent's sense of security and level of maturity. The most important responsibility of the custodial/visitation arrangement is supporting the child's time with and exposure to the other parent; at the same time, the most painful experience of that arrangement is a result of that support—the sense of rejection.

The other major responsibilities of the custodial parent revolve around health, education, and religion. Because of the amount of

time the child spends in the custodial home, proper medical attention, academic pursuits, and spiritual involvement are largely the
responsibility of the custodial parent. The role of the parent with
visitation rights is more one of supporting these activities—emotionally and perhaps financially—rather than carrying them out.

If raising children is a difficult task in today's society, then
raising children of divorce is twice as difficult. It works best when
there is a cooperative working relationship between the ex-
spouses. The very nature of this arrangement is complex, the
expectation being that two people who have not gotten along and
consequently have gotten divorced will now work well together.
The situation is eased somewhat by the fact that the actual process of the custodial/visitation situation does not require a lot of
contact between ex-partners. The day-to-day reality of living this
experience is between parent and child, not parent and parent. As
you get farther into this book, the common pitfalls and problems
of living with custody and visitation after divorce will be spelled
out. Avoiding these common problems and following these simple
precepts will make a difficult situation workable.

The Courts and the Custody Issue

The role the courts prefer to take in divorce is one of protecting
the rights of both adults and at the same time sanctioning the
agreement that the adults have worked out through negotiations
with their attorneys. If divorce takes place in this fashion there
is very little time actually spent in court, and practically no decisions for the judge to make.

The role courts detest is serving as referee between two angry
adults who project all the bitterness and resentment from a
broken marriage onto the divorce settlement and ultimately force
the court into a position of imposing its decision because of the
lack of conciliation on the part of the couple. Divorce often brings
out the irrational side of adults. It makes logical decisions difficult
and often leaves both adults feeling that these decisions are unfair
or unjust. "Why should I have to give up my house because he
wanted to play around? He was the one who wanted out of the

marriage" is a common complaint heard in courtrooms across the country. If allowed, "who did what to whom" would be a never-ending game in the courtroom. Therefore fair and equitable settlements are based more on length of marriage, assets acquired during the marriage, and the ability to provide for self and others after the divorce.

Least popular of all is the battle over custody. The court prefers avoiding decisions in this area because the issues involved are outside its area of expertise. A person with a background in child development, psychology, and family systems is needed to make the decisions. Consequently it is often difficult for the court to distinguish between the legitimate custody disputes and those cases in which custody is only a bargaining chip in an attempt to achieve a better financial settlement. In the latter situation the court feels manipulated and used. Yet even the former situation is not without problems. How to determine the best custodial alternative, what to do if both parents are equally competent, what to do if both parents have significant liabilities, where the wishes of the child fit in—these are some of the decisions that face the court.

Limited in its ability to resolve these questions and others, the court most often deals with the custody dispute either by getting outside professional help (see "What Is Mediation and Its Role in Custody Determination?") or using a simple formula. The formula is that the children go to the parent who has been most responsible for their day-to-day care unless the other parent can prove that the first parent is incompetent in some major way to carry out these responsibilities (issues of competency are dealt with in the next chapter). Consequently there still exists in the court system a decided preference toward maternal custody.

The Role of the Attorney

Your attorney's role is to obtain for you the best settlement possible under the laws of the state in which you reside. His job is to interpret those laws and apply them to your marital situation. The laws are sometimes specific but more often only define parameters for settlements. Some states, for example, have precise laws on what percentage of income is to be given for child support, while other states are more vague. Inside these parameters lawyers argue on behalf of their clients.

If laws governing settlement are usually general, then laws governing custody decisions are practically nonexistent. This situation results in more room for interpretation and argument within the legal structure. What becomes admissible evidence can be and often is extensive. Consequently custody disputes that go to trial are frequently long-drawn-out, expensive proceedings. What most people don't realize is that, unless there is sufficient evidence to override the natural inclination of the court (see preceding section), then all the testimony becomes a wasted exercise. Attorneys are aware of this, but they are caught in a bind. If a client says, "I want to go for custody. I think I'm the best parent," the attorney has an ethical obligation to obtain the best settlement possible under the law. If there aren't specific statutes that define custody disputes, then regardless of what the attorney knows is likely to be the eventual outcome, he is obligated to pursue custody for his client.

Most attorneys will inform their clients of the likelihood, or lack thereof, of obtaining custody. However, in the face of pressure by clients they will not, nor should they, refuse to press the issue. Furthermore, many clients caught in the angry emotions of divorce will unconsciously or even purposely distort the truth. This of course will lead many attorneys to believe they have a winnable case until the battle is engaged and the depositions and hearings begin. Even then it often takes some time and a great deal of probing on both sides to determine where the distortions exist.

There is a system that the courts are gradually turning toward that will help custody disputes climb out of this morass of distortion, one-upmanship, lengthy depositions, hearings, and trials. To be sure, it won't eliminate trials; nevertheless, it will shorten the length of time custody disputes take, make sense out of much of the distortion, be based more on the needs of the children than on the rights of the adults (without violating those rights), and in general be a more efficient mechanism for resolving these disputes. Therefore fewer disputes will go to trial. The judges will be not have to make as many custody determinations, and when they must, they will have the kind of information that is most helpful. The system is called mediation.

What Is Mediation and Its Role in Custody Determination?

For many years attorneys have been using psychologists, psychiatrists, and to a lesser extent social workers to testify in support of their clients' attempts to acquire custody. The courts for the most part have welcomed these contributions. These professionals added the psychological expertise that the courts were lacking. With this expertise judges had more basis on which to make their determinations. However, there was no definite structure in which these professionals could perform. What frequently occurred was that the mother and children would be evaluated by one professional, and the father and children by another. Then, in court, the judge could listen to two psychologists with different views instead of two parents with different views. Occasionally the two attorneys would agree on a single professional to do the evaluation. Frequently, however, after the evaluation found in one parent's favor, the opposing attorney would seek a second opinion or get a second professional to criticize the findings of the first. The result was that, despite the professional opinions, the arguments continued, and little has been done to keep the battle out of the courtroom.

In the early 1980s mediation became popular. Initially it was a process by which couples would attempt to agree to a financial settlement with an impartial third party (not either of their attorneys). This mediator might be a social worker or a third attorney. The mediator would attempt to separate the marital bitterness from the settlement process and then negotiate back and forth until all the financial issues were agreed upon. The process was fairly successful; therefore, it began to be attempted with custody disputes as well.

In contrast to mediation ordered by the court, voluntary medi-

ation of custody disputes has been a failure. In financial mediation, there are things to trade: "I'll give you this bank account for
the car," for example. In custodial mediation there is nothing to
trade for the children. The only time successful mediation occurred would be when bitterness would dissipate and the couple
themselves could logically agree on what was in the best interests
of the children.

What has begun to emerge is a combination of the two processes described above: psychological evaluation and mediation. It
has been moderately successful resolving custody disputes while
at the same time very helpful to the judges when it remains necessary for them to make custody determinations. In a few places,
for example, several counties in Illinois, statutes have been written into law creating a mandatory mediation/evaluation program.
These statutes require that all cases of dispute of custody or visitation be turned over to a mediator who is a licensed psychologist.
The statute is enacted by court order after the first petitions for
divorce are filed revealing the custody dispute.

Mediation, with the court order, has been very successful. In a
prescribed number of sessions the psychologist sees the divorcing
couple, the children, and various combinations of children and
adults. In the beginning sessions an attempt is made to help the
couple themselves agree on custody. Because of the court's order
there is more cooperation with this process than would otherwise
occur. The result is that most of the cases are mediated. For those
that are not, the psychologist makes recommendations to the
court concerning who would be the best custodial parent. These
recommendations are based on the information gathered in the
sessions, psychological testing that has been done, and perhaps
consultation with agencies or people connected with the family
(e.g., schools, hospitals, doctors, etc.). The process is professional
and efficient. The court order makes it effective. The result is that
fewer and fewer cases of custody come to trial. Furthermore, custody cases that are mediated are less likely to come back to court
as postdecree problems.

Chapter 2

Going Through Divorce:
Issues of Custody and Visitation

Making Your Own Custody Decision

There are many reasons why couples get divorced. Financial problems, problems with in-laws, sexual problems, poor communication, differences of opinion about how to raise children, religious differences—the list is long. Most couples who get divorced have many of these problems, not just one or two. They begin to overwhelm the couple, destroying the fabric of specialness that originally created the love and desire for marriage. As the divorce unfolds, often the arguments around these problems intensify. For example, couples who fight about money while they're married are likely to have trouble agreeing on financial settlements in their divorce. Too often the anger and resentments spill over into areas that previously were not issues of conflict. To extend the battle in this way is painful, harmful for everyone, and expensive—often attorneys are asked to resolve problems that didn't previously exist in the marriage.

If you didn't disagree about how to raise your children during the marriage, then don't fight over them in your divorce. If you thought you were both good parents during the marriage, then don't put down the parenting skills of your spouse during the divorce. The pain of leaving the children is often the worst part of getting divorced. Don't try to ease your pain—or perhaps your guilt—by stirring up a custody battle without excellent reasons.

The children suffer. Remember, you'll work through your pain, and your adjustment will be a lot easier than theirs.

Make your decisions about custody and visitation before making decisions about the financial settlement.

Decisions about custody and visitation should be made on the principle that what is in the best interests of the children is to keep as much of their life intact as possible. It is traumatic enough that they will not be living with both of you together anymore.

Keep the children in the same house or apartment they have been living in if financially possible.

If you must leave the house or apartment, keep the children in the same school district.

The custodial arrangement should mirror family life as much as possible. The parent who is the primary caretaker of the children should remain the primary caretaker *and* have custody. If both parents are active in this capacity, then one should have custody and frequent visitation should be scheduled for the other. See Chapter 5 for a test that will help determine who is the more active caretaker.

Despite what seems to be a simple decision in most cases, I still see parents in dispute because, even though the father travels during the week and the mother is there on a daily basis, the father is asking for custody. Perhaps the children are boys, and on weekends he plays ball with his sons and takes them places. He feels he has a close relationship with his children; calls them when he is on the road; spends time with them when he is home. He feels therefore that he should have custody, even if the children have to be with a housekeeper or grandparents while he travels. Clearly this man's motivation is fear of losing his children through divorce, guilt that he has been out of the home as much as he has, and ignorance that visitation can be established which will provide both him and his children the same level of involvement they had in the intact family. As long as mom is competent, there really is no alternative to maternal custody.

Remember, when there are no serious questions about parenting ability, keep the divorced environment for the children as similar to the original family environment as possible.

Custody of Infants and Preschoolers

Children under school age, in the vast majority of cases, belong with their mothers. The rule is that life after the divorce should mirror as closely as possible family life prior to the divorce. The majority of infants and preschoolers have been nurtured and tended to by their mothers and therefore should remain with them.

I know many men who have taken an active role in the care and nurturing of their infants. They have bathed and diapered, prepared formulas, and gotten up in the middle of the night with a teething or sick child. While fathers like these may still be a minority, their numbers are significant and growing. However, occasional or even frequent attention to these activities is not the same as that which is typically provided by the mother. The bonding is usually greater with the mother than with the father, and custody should be set up accordingly. To interfere with the primary bonding of the mother and child at these early ages is to cause severe trauma to the child. Such interference is to be avoided at all costs unless the mother is physically or mentally incapable of fulfilling parenting responsibilities.

What Is Typical or Normal Visitation?

Every other weekend from Friday after school or evening until Sunday after dinner, and one night a week for approximately two to three hours, is a typical visitation schedule. This can be increased or decreased some depending on the needs and wants of the children and the availability of the parents. Yet it is a good basic schedule and has benefits for everyone.

Every other weekend means that on a regular basis the noncustodial parent has the children sleeping in his/her home. There is the opportunity to tuck the children in at night and wake up with them in the morning. Visiting one weeknight a week means that never more than a week goes by that children won't see their other parent. This schedule allows children to visit the noncustodial parent for at least ten days a month. If the parent takes advantage of this schedule it is more than enough time to maintain the quality of their relationship and have influence over the growth and development of the children.

This visitation schedule is also beneficial for the parents' private lives. Every other weekend they can focus on responsibilities other than the children and can be with friends, date, go away for the weekend, etc. Single parenting, even with the support of an ex-spouse, is a difficult job. Rest and relaxation time is needed. It is available in this visitation schedule.

Sometimes circumstances call for alterations in this schedule. Preschool children should see the noncustodial parent more frequently—two nights every week for two hours a night in addition to every other weekend is recommended.

When parents work weekends or parts of weekends, the typical visitation schedule also needs to be altered. Splitting every weekend in half is one solution; the noncustodial parent having three Saturday nights and Sundays and the custodial parent having the rest of those weekends and one full weekend per month is another possibility. Don't be afraid to try different arrangements, and ask the children what they like. Any arrangement that allows children to visit the other parent between six and twelve days per month will sustain parental bonding, involvement, and influence.

How Holidays and Vacations Fit into Custody/Visitation

The typical and normal schedule for holidays is to alternate them throughout the year and rotate them every other year. There are seven major holidays a year: New Year's, Easter, Memorial Day, Fourth of July, Labor Day, Thanksgiving, and Christmas. Regardless of who has custody the following schedule is typical: Mother has the children New Year's, Memorial Day, Labor Day, and Christmas in even-numbered years (1990, 1992, etc.) and father has the children on those same holidays in odd-numbered years (1991, 1993, etc.); while in odd-numbered years mother has the children on Easter, Fourth of July, and Thanksgiving and the children are with their father on those holidays in even-numbered years. Important religious holidays can be added to the rotation and dealt with by the same method. Parents can agree to a different schedule if certain holidays are more important to one and different holidays are more important to the other. This is suggested as a fair and equitable solution to any arguing over holidays that might occur.

In addition, mothers should always have their children on Mother's Day and fathers on Father's Day. I recommend that no special arrangement be made for the children on their birthdays, rather they should spend the day wherever they are according to the normal visitation schedule. As it is in our society, children often celebrate their birthdays both on the day itself and on the weekend closest to their birthday, thus making it possible for children of divorce to celebrate their birthdays with both of their parents.

Where there is typical and normal visitation, I recommend three weeks of vacation with the children for both parents. This means three weeks of time uninterrupted by visitation from the other parent. It is suggested that the noncustodial parent take one week of vacation during the three weeks that the children get time off at Christmas and spring break and two weeks during the summer. This does not mean the parent must take the children away during these periods—merely that the parent has uninterrupted time with them. Where the usual visitation schedule is not possible, as in situations where parents live in different cities, a different vacation schedule may be appropriate.

Where Should the Noncustodial Parent Live?

Stay in the children's school district if at all possible. If the children stay in the marital home, it is beneficial to everyone for the other parent to find a place to live in the same school district. If both parents move, the rule is still the same. Both parents should attempt to stay in the original school district. This will mean that there is never a long drive to visit mom or dad. It will also eliminate arguments about who should do the driving, because the distance is short enough that it won't matter. It will also mean that when the children visit the other parent they don't necessarily leave their friends. This makes visitation more fun for the children—they don't feel they are giving things up—and is less burdensome for the parents—they don't feel they must entertain the kids every minute they are with them. In this way visitation approximates normal family living.

This arrangement will probably not last forever. However, it is an excellent transition from married family life to single-parent life. It eases the change for both children and adults. Eventually job changes and remarriages will create situations that pull one parent or the other farther away. Still, it is advisable to stay within a half-hour driving distance from your children. Longer distances than this create situations in which it becomes increasingly likely for visitation to be missed. The greatest suffering then is the children's.

What Is Full Joint Custody?

The term *full joint custody* refers to an arrangement in which, for example, one parent has the children three days a week and the other parent has them four days a week; the number of days is reversed the next week. Another joint custody arrangement would be to have the children one full week in one parent's home and the next full week in the other parent's home. This type of custody arrangement satisfies parental needs, but it does not satisfy the needs of the children. Furthermore, regardless of how well the divorcing parents get along, it is a difficult situation to set up and maintain. I have never seen it work well for long periods of time, and even children who don't want to make choices between one parent and another don't like the arrangement. They dislike the constant going back and forth, they are unhappy that their friends never know where to find them, and they are confused by the different rules and responsibilities in the two homes. They dislike the constant readjustment to the different temperaments and parenting styles in the two homes. And finally, they dislike the continual packing and unpacking, or discovering that an outfit they want to wear to school is at the other home. Psychologically they lose their sense of home.

If by now you aren't convinced to avoid joint custody, then at the very least, follow these rules. Both parents must live in the same school district. The children should have enough clothes to have wardrobes at both houses, or at least enough to keep packing and unpacking to a minimum. Parents must agree on responsibilities they give the children, emphasis they put on grades, policies they set on social life and extracurricular activities, and the type and severity of discipline they impose. Obviously, this system requires a great deal of contact between the parents. And finally, if you do manage to work it all out, know that it will probably come undone as soon as one of you remarries.

The only situation in which this custodial arrangement tends to work is for preschool children. Their world is small—peers are still a peripheral part of their lives—and their focus remains within the family, on parents and siblings. When children start first grade, a more definitive custodial decision is needed.

What Is Residential or Physical Custody with Joint Custody?

This term refers to one parent having physical custody of the children while both parents take decision-making responsibility for major issues of health and education. The residential or physical custodian makes all the day-to-day decisions regarding hygiene, bedtime, friends, TV, homework, etc. The two parents make joint decisions regarding issues of elective surgery, orthodontia, private schools, or special education. There are still custodial and noncustodial parents, but the latter have a sense that they have more of a say in the life of their children. In fact, they do, and at some point in the raising of the children, joint decisions will be required. Only parents who are fully vested in the visitation schedule should be part of this kind of custodial arrangement.

Should the Children Be Split Up?

Another general rule is that the children should not be split up in divorce. Sometimes, in an attempt to deal with one parent's sense of loss or to keep the dispute out of the courts, children will be dealt with like property: "You can have these two if I can have this one." If, however, you follow the rule "Life after divorce should mirror the family situation prior to divorce," then all the children stay together. It is difficult enough for a child to have lessened contact with one of his or her parents without having to deal with the sense of loss and/or jealousy created by having a sibling living with the other parent.

This rule will dominate in the majority of divorces. However, there are enough exceptions to the rule that some of the more common reasons for splitting up the children should be discussed. Sometimes a bad marriage continues for years, and as the children grow they are exposed to the marital discord and fights. Frequently they will side with one parent. In some cases two children will side with different parents. The siding often involves some identification with the parent. When this happens, there is also disappointment in and even anger toward the other parent. If this siding is not interfered with by the parents, a strong attachment will develop. Results of the test in Chapter 5 may indicate that it is more appropriate for one or more of the children to go with one parent and one or more of the children to go with the other. Incidentally, such children will need some help in reattaching to and forgiving the other parent.

In some families without this type of identification, there may be other kinds of attachments between children and parents that make a split appropriate. For example, a thirteen-year-old boy who is very into his male identification with his father and their activities may appropriately go with dad while his ten-year-old sister stays with mom. Caution is urged in these situations, however. Children should not automatically be assigned to the like-sex parent. Attachment and the ability to care for the child should be the deciding factors.

The final exception is the situation in which either the would-be custodial parent can't control one of the children or a destructive sibling rivalry necessitates separating the children. This last situation more commonly takes place after the divorce and therefore is discussed more thoroughly in Chapter 4.

How Much Should Children's Wishes Influence the Decision?

Children should not decide custody. Custody is always an adult decision. Children's wants are not always healthy—for example, some children will eat candy until they are sick. They may want the candy, but it's not good for them. Custody should be a well-thought-out decision based on a multitude of rational factors. Children of any age are not capable of making such a decision.

Children should not be asked which parent they want to live with, for this is asking them to choose between two people they love. Both the division of loyalty and the possession of that kind of power are unhealthy at that age. Furthermore, if a child is forced to make that decision, the guilt regarding the other parent will be substantial: In the acceptance of one parent there is the rejection of the other. This is clearly not in the child's best interests.

Nevertheless the children's wishes and wants are important. They need to be paid attention to. Listening carefully to the children will help determine to whom they are more attached. "I want to live with dad because he plays catch with me and takes me to ball games" is an indication of one level of attachment. "I talk to mom whenever I have a problem" indicates a deeper level of attachment that involves support, help with problem-solving, learning values, and understanding feelings. A "doing things" relationship is more superficial than a communication-based relationship. However, both are important, and both need to be considered when establishing the custodial and visitation arrangements.

In summary, don't ask your kids with whom they want to live. If they tell you their preference, appreciate their request but let them know it's an adult decision. Remember that the kind and quality of the child-adult relationship is the key to making custodial decisions.

When You Can't Decide on Custody

Seek mediation. If you live in a county where mediation is part of the structure of the court system, you will be referred to a mediator through court order. Otherwise, seek the services of a private mediator. Your attorneys can recommend someone. It should be someone whom neither one of you knows and has no allegiance to either attorney. It should be someone with experience in custody evaluation and mediation and, if the state has licensing to cover the process, someone who is licensed. Typically this person is a psychologist. In some states it may be a social worker.

Both parents should initially be seen together for one or two sessions. Then each parent should be seen once individually. The children should be seen alone, and each parent should be seen separately with the children. More joint sessions may follow, and psychological testing may be useful. In all, unless you reach an agreement during the process, as many as ten sessions over a two-month period may be necessary to complete the mediation. If agreement has not been reached at the end of this time, the mediator will have enough information to give you and the court recommendations on custody and visitation. The mediator should either be paid a retainer in advance, or you should sign a written agreement on how much of the mediation each will pay for. This is done in advance so as not to influence the outcome of the mediation.

Mediation and the Decision Process

The mediator will first explain to both of you the process of mediation. Next he will encourage you to talk about your marriage and the children. He will ask the whys and wherefores of the divorce if they are not already obvious. The mediator will elicit conversation about custody and why each of you feels you are the best custodial alternative. He will help you distinguish between your needs to have custody and what is in the best interests of your children. He will attempt to separate your anger, bitterness, and blaming from the custody issue. He will help you understand the difference between a bad spouse and a bad parent and point out that the two aren't necessarily synonymous. And if he's able to accomplish all of this, it is more than likely he will be able to help the two of you agree on who is the best custodial choice.

If he is not successful at this, he will continue to meet with the different members of the family in an effort to cut through the false claims and distortions and make recommendations to you and the court about custody. Like the court, he will be guided by what the family attachments were prior to the breakdown of the marriage. He will seek to determine which parent the children are more emotionally attached to; which parent is more emotionally available; which parent is more physically available; who has more common sense; who is willing to admit they don't have all the answers; who is willing to ask questions; and more.

In some situations one parent is the clear choice, and the decision is easy. Sometimes, however, both parents are more or less equal, or the strengths and attachments of one parent are offset by the strengths and attachments of the other. The decision then is far more complicated.

Sometimes parents will try to manipulate the situation or directly influence their children. This is obvious to the mediator and is sometimes held against such parents. Frequently a father, fearful of losing his children in divorce, will become Superdad after it's announced that a divorce will take place. Helping the children with their homework, going places on weekends, and otherwise being available is a common response. If it wasn't the norm long before the divorce was announced, this behavior won't have much influence on the decision, although it does point to the potential and capacity of the father to be with his children in a meaningful way. More subtle and direct manipulations of the children are frequently witnessed. When a ten-year-old informs the mediator, "Dad is trying to buy my love" or "Dad isn't giving mom the child support money," the mediator is aware that attempts are being made by the mother to manipulate the children. "Dad is trying to buy my love" is simply not a concept children come up with on their own.

After all the information and data are gathered, a report is prepared. The mediator should meet with the parents, without the children, and give them his recommendations and the reasons for those recommendations. The written report is then submitted to the attorneys and the court. Often the couple will agree to the custodial recommendations of the mediator even if they haven't agreed during the mediation process itself. However, if they don't agree, the mediation process and the mediator's report do not supplant the individual's rights to a trial.

Competent/Incompetent versus Desirable/Undesirable Parents

Parents frequently present themselves in mediation in such a way as to suggest that the other parent is incompetent. However, what spouses consider incompetent is more often simply reflective of a difference in parenting styles. A parent who feels it's important to adhere to a strict bedtime may consider the other parent lax when he or she allows the child to stay up late. In an attempt to portray themselves as the good parent, I have repeatedly heard parents complain about their spouse's stance on sweets, winter clothing, brushing teeth, bedtime, and more. Of course it is important to pay attention to the physical well-being of the children, but a preoccupation with these issues to the exclusion of the equally important relationship issues is always curious. Furthermore, rigid adherence to the above-mentioned concerns often points to a lack of the flexibility that is essential to good parenting and calls into question the parenting ability of the protesting adult.

Essentially there are two issues involved. One is competence—whether a parent's behavior makes him or her incompetent to be a custodial parent. A determination of incompetence is based on the existence of some potential for significant physical or emotional harm to the children. Concerns about physical abuse, sexual abuse, criminal behavior, and neglect or abandonment through alcoholism, drug abuse, or severe emotional illness are part of the competence/incompetence issue. If these concerns are validated, then that parent should not have custody.

The other issue is one of desirability—whether a parent's behavior makes him or her undesirable to be a custodial parent. This determination is based on ability to adequately meet the children's emotional and physical needs. Whether a parent gets up in the morning to make breakfast for the children, is available to help with homework, is supportive of the children's relationship with the other parent, is capable of a communicative relationship with the children and monitors the children's hygiene, diet, and other physical well-being concerns—all these questions are part of the desirable/undesirable parent issue.

Most disputes over custody center around each parent's desirability as a custodian. In this arena most of the disputes are about levels of desirability—seldom is one parent clearly desirable and the other parent clearly undesirable. If this is the case the parents themselves are usually aware of it and the decision about custody is made between them.

What is a more difficult "call'" is the choice between an undesirable and an incompetent parent. If the incompetence is due to a treatable condition like substance abuse or mental problems and the undesirability is due to an inability to nurture, then perhaps a temporary custodial arrangement is needed until treatment is successful for the incompetent parent. It might be this parent who would emerge in the long run as the best custodial alternative. Some undesirable parents can be helped through education: for example, parenting classes. Parents who are either incompetent or undesirable need professional help before they can take an active role with their children.

Changing Schools

Regardless of our attempts to keep life the same for our children, financial considerations sometimes make it impossible. Selling the family home may be necessary for both adults to survive. If this occurs it is best to stay within the same school district. Losing their sense of family is painful for children; losing a sense of home is painful; and keeping these losses to a minimum is important. Nevertheless, sometimes a mother or father with custody will want to move across school districts for financial reasons or perhaps to be closer to their own nuclear family. When this occurs, move during the school year.

Yes, that's right, move during the school year. Educators will tell you the best time to start a child in a new school is at the beginning of a school year. Academically, there is some validity to this. The child starts with his class. Testing and placement can occur prior to the start of classes and it is easier in general for the school administration. But it is easier emotionally for the child if the transfer is made during the school year. At the beginning of school, all of the kids who haven't seen each other for two months are getting reacquainted and catching up with each other. Your children will hardly be noticed and may have a difficult time breaking in. However, if your children transfer during the year, they will be the new kids in class and everyone will want to get to know them. The transition will be a lot easier.

Blame for the Divorce

"It's his fault." "It's all her fault."

Husbands and wives invariably disagree about what has destroyed their marriage. Most everybody blames the other person for the divorce. While their perceptions are often self-serving, both adults are probably right to some degree. Understanding one's own responsibility for divorce is important for the individual. One-upmanship in this area, however, is pointless, and if the children are exposed to it, it can cause serious harm.

Children are very perceptive. They find out all on their own what their parents are like and what their strengths and weaknesses are. To blame your spouse in front of your children does two things: First, it forces the children to take sides and divide their loyalties; second, it stirs up the children's anger.

Remember how you felt when you were a child and someone at school belittled your mother or father. You felt open anger toward that person. When you belittle your spouse—even for good reason—your children will experience anger toward you. It may be conscious or unconscious. If you mount a campaign against your spouse, even if it's effective now, it will eventually backfire and cause considerable pain for your children. If you are effective in interfering with your children's relationship with their other parent, you will (1) create pain, (2) remove that parent as a person for the children to receive love from, (3) remove that parent as a source of identification for the children, and (4) create guilt for your children. Eventually the children will turn on you and be furious because you interfered with their relationship with the other parent. In essence you are trading off exclusive closeness with your children now for the possibility of no closeness later on. The entire situation is abusive to the children.

The point on which this all turns is the word *exclusive.* When a couple separates, they divide up all that in the past they shared—except the children. Everything else they have exclusive ownership over, but when it comes to the children they need to share—share responsibility and share their love.

Never complain about your spouse to your children. Never blame your spouse in front of the children. Never blame your spouse in conversation with other people where your children can hear. The end result is always emotional trauma for the child and the disruption of all of the child-parent relationships.

This rule holds true even when the other parent is incompetent and clearly more to blame. Even a child of an alcoholic or a child who has experienced physical abuse at the hands of a parent wants that parent's love and wants a relationship with that parent. The kind and quality of that relationship needs to be worked out by the child and parent without coercion by the other parent. As soon as there is interference the child's loyalties are divided and the trauma begins. The children themselves need to see that their other parent is "bad" and make their choices accordingly. "I don't want to visit mom 'cause she always drinks when I come over" is much different from "I don't want you to go to your mother's because she's a drunk."

If left to draw their own conclusions, children are more capable than divorcing spouses of simultaneously seeing the good and bad in each. They will acknowledge that a parent has problems but that they love that parent despite those problems; that maybe they won't spend as much time with that parent, but that they love him or her nonetheless. Divorcing spouses tend to see things in terms of black and white, good or bad, but trying to influence children into this line of thought damages their natural bonding to their parents.

Divorcing Partners: If We Get Along, Can We Get Together?

Often I'm asked by divorcing couples if they can get together with the children as a couple while the divorce is in progress. I always turn the question around and inquire about their motives. If they are actually trying to put the marriage back together, I instruct them to put the divorce on hold and get into marital therapy. Most often, however, the motive for getting together is simply one of easing the transition for the children. The intentions are good, but misguided.

Doing things as a family after the separation helps the children deny the reality of divorce. It creates unrealistic hope in them that their parents will get back together again. This is a natural wish on their part. Most children have a conscious or unconscious wish for the family unit to remain intact and for everyone to live happily ever after. Getting together as a family merely enlivens that wish and interferes with the children's need to pick up the pieces and move forward. It also encourages the children to make attempts themselves at getting mom and dad together. It is a focus and a burden that is unhealthy for them.

Some couples continue to get together even after the divorce is over. They are proud of the fact that they can get along and believe that the family get-togethers are good for the children. In fact, this practice is even worse than the getting together during the divorce process. It has all the same negatives for the children, and negatives for the parents as well. Eventually other adults will come into the picture—as friends, as dates, or as lovers and potential mates. These adults will be viewed by the children and possibly the ex-spouse as intruders into the dream of the reunited family. The children are likely to respond negatively to them and angrily to you; after all, you're "cheating" on the other parent. The fact that you have kept the dream alive has them feeling as if you are cheating regardless of the divorce. The children then are forced to deal with their negative responses to nice people, their angry feelings toward you, and the resultant feelings of guilt. Consequently, when you've decided to get divorced and you've separated, don't get back together again for "family time." It's not in the children's best interests.

Children's Knowledge of the Settlement

There's no useful purpose served by the children knowing the details of the divorce settlement. For older children, "who gets what" will become obvious as the divorce is finalized. To expose the children to the parameters of debt, division of assets, and details of child support is to invite them to judge the fairness of the settlement and to take sides. This process falls in the same category as blaming, and for all the reasons discussed earlier in this chapter, it should be avoided. Instead of comments like "You can't get those jeans because your father won't give me enough money," it should be "The divorce is making things tight for both dad and me, and you'll have to wait on those new jeans." Financial issues are adult matters, and children should not be exposed to them.

Guilt, and Guilt About Noncustody

Often parents who don't take or get custody feel guilty about their decision or the court's action. Guilt is experienced when your behavior doesn't measure up to your expectations of yourself. Sometimes societal pressures add to this burden of guilt. For example, it is expected that women should want and fight for custody of their children. If the father gets custody, many women feel guilty, regardless of how appropriate the custodial arrangements are. Some fathers will fight for custody of their children because they want the children to know they are wanted. They may have initiated the divorce and feel guilty that they have created so much disruption in the children's lives. They will make it up to them, they believe, if they have custody. Guilt about the disruption surfaces if they don't obtain custody. Guilt over non-custody for either parent is an understandable but also unnecessary burden. It is painful and only adds to an already difficult situation. It will drain your energy and affect your ability to work and to take pleasure in life.

Some guilt is healthy. It can be a signal that your selfish concerns are superseding the needs of your children. If this guilt is paid attention to and responded to, it should dissipate as corrective action is taken. Guilt in general about the children is to be expected. To some degree every divorcing parent experiences it. After all, you have disrupted their lives. However, if the divorcing process is not destructive to your children and fosters their ability to deal with things, then the guilt should dissipate as you see them coping. If guilt lingers or turns into self-pity, professional help is needed. It often takes an objective outsider to help you see which guilt is appropriate and which is unrealistic.

Abandonment

All of us realize that two parents working cooperatively in a custody-and-visitation arrangement in which each parent feels and executes responsibility for the moral, educational, and psychological growth of their children is an ideal. Sometimes other things happen to kids on the way to adulthood. Abandonment by one or both parents is a possible sequel to divorce and can become a major life event with which the children may have to cope. A child may need to go through psychotherapy in order to deal with what has happened and salvage his or her self-esteem.

Some adults will not only divorce their spouses but in effect will divorce their children also. In so doing, they abandon them. Sometimes it may be because they feel guilty over an affair. Sometimes parents of very young children will concoct excuses to stay away from their kids. They rationalize that the children are so young that the parent's disappearance won't affect them. The children won't remember them. Or it will be confusing for the children to have stepparents and biological parents, so they'll make it easier by disappearing. These are all rationalizations that serve the selfish needs of the parent. Unless children are going to be harmed by a parent, there is never a justification for abandonment. Children are unable to see the selfish needs in adult behavior and invariably take abandonment personally. It is always an affront to their self-esteem and sense of worth. Hidden in their adult personalities is often the persistent question, "What was wrong with me that made my parent leave?" The job of the remaining parent (or other relative if both parents disappear) is to give the child a sense of being wanted and loved, a sense that the child is a wonderful addition to their life and not a burden. This may best be accomplished with professional psychological help.

Occasionally parents who have disappeared will return, sometimes three or four years later. The natural inclination is not to allow them to have contact with the child. The thinking is understandable; why allow them to hurt the child again? In most cases, however, the thinking is wrong. To begin with, the decision in most states will be a legal one. If the court says visitation should be initiated, then aside from any legal recourse, you must allow the parental contact. As long as the absent parent's intentions are genuine, children will, for the most part, respond favorably. They have a curiosity about the missing parent. They have a desire to understand what happened and they have a need to feel accepted. They also then have someone real to attach their abandonment feelings to, ask questions of, become more knowledgeable about— consequently, if they should be abandoned again, they will be better able to deal with the loss. Abandonment is tragic for children, but if dealt with properly by the adults who remain behind, it is survivable.

Chapter 3

Living With Custody
and Visitation After Divorce

How the System Should Work

The majority of divorced couples without children have little if anything to do with each other after the divorce is concluded. If they live in the same town or community, they may on occasion run into each other, but frequently, years may go by without contact. Many others simply never see or hear from each other again. However, if you have children, you have a tie that binds you together regardless of your preferences. The link is tighter when the children are young and becomes looser as the children grow. But even when the children are grown, occasions like graduation from college, marriage, and the birth of children (your grandchildren) will pull you back together.

Since most ex-spouses, given the choice, would prefer to lead separate lives, the involvement with each other created by the necessity and desire to raise the children can be difficult. Yet following some simple rules, with the understanding that neither one of you relishes the contact, can allow the arrangements to work quite smoothly.

In the following examples, maternal custody with paternal visitation will be assumed. This is not meant to imply a preference for this custodial arrangement; paternal custody is definitely on the increase in this country, but maternal custody is still the arrangement for the vast majority of children. Whether it is sole custody or maternal residential custody with joint custody doesn't matter; the procedures apply in both cases.

When the children are over the age of ten, the ex-spouses' contact can be minimal. Once regular visitation is established, the contact can be between father and children. Reconfirming of pickup time and place can be made by phone. If the ex-wife answers, a simple, "How are you? I'm fine, thank you. I've called to talk to Mike. Is he available?" is all that is necessary. The vast majority of the time there are few if any issues that require extensive ex-spouse communication. Even discussion of report cards and school performance takes place between parent and child rather than parent and parent. Consequently, with reasonably well-adjusted children the amount of parent-to-parent contact should be minimal. An occasional call to shorten or lengthen a visit or share some important news about the children or that may affect them is all that is necessary.

Parents need to talk if school performance becomes a concern. However, a bad grade here or there should not be used as an excuse to call the former spouse and question her ability to raise the children. Poor school performance or social adjustment should be a concern for both parents and does not automatically mean that there are problems in the custodial home.

For children under the age of ten, more regular contact will be needed. Younger children have more difficulty with time concepts and figuring out how many and what kind of clothes to take for weekend visits. They need help from their parents. Consequently, their parents need to talk. The younger the children are, the greater the need for contact.

Children of all ages will frequently have commitments that conflict with visitation. For children over ten I recommend they discuss these occasions directly with the father. The priority is visitation. Often, however, with a little flexibility, the event and visitation can be squeezed in on one weekend. Everyone gets what they want, and the father's flexibility will endear him to the child. Occasionally the event will mean skipping visitation altogether or switching weekends. Again, this needs to be worked out between the child and the father.

With younger children, such arrangements need to be worked

out between the parents. Extracurricular activities and occasions like friends' birthday parties and family events cannot interfere with visitation. Occasionally visiting can be missed, but every effort should be made to see that this does not occur. Music lessons and after-school pursuits such as Cub Scouts, Girl Scouts, and sports are wonderful activities that serve to help make children well-rounded, but they too must be worked into the custodial/visitation arrangement. One of the most important priorities of any custodial arrangment is ensuring that the children have time with the noncustodial parent. Regardless of opinions about the ex-spouse's parenting skills, parents are not entitled to interfere with their children's need and desire to have two parents in their lives.

Respecting these guidelines will help in your children's adjustment and minimize the contact between parents. Understanding the children's needs for contact with both their parents as well as their friends and avoiding parental selfishness that ignores the children's needs will also help. Remember, children get bad grades, break arms, and get sick in intact families also. These occasional events do not in and of themselves justify criticism of the other parent or threats of going back to court. Their occurrence should only precipitate parental concern about the well-being and feelings of the child.

Children need sharing and acknowledgment from their parents. Listening to their stories from the other parent's home with interest and compassion will only serve to enhance your own relationship with your children. If you turn a deaf ear or react jealously to the account of the wonderful time the kids had with the other parent, then they will stop talking about it (unless they want to upset you). If you threaten to annihilate the other parent when you hear that he or she was unfair or favored a sibling or punished too severely, you will similarly turn off communication. Children don't want retribution against someone they love, they just want these feelings understood and acknowledged.

Gifts: Children Giving—Children Getting

Children's gift giving and receiving can be especially difficult for some divorced parents. Watching their children gleefully open presents sent by the ex-spouse, listening to their children talk to friends and neighbors about the wonderful gift dad sent, or watching them shop for a present for their dad are situations that can promote jealousy, anger, and resentment in the most secure mother. If this happens, birthdays, Christmas, Mother's and Father's Day all become events filled with tension.

Gift giving and receiving should be viewed as loving exchanges between parent and child. If this is kept in mind, it will diminish the jealous responses. Perhaps you will even be able to share in your child's enthusiasm. But whether or not you can do this, you must share in the process—for the child's sake. For example, if you don't take your child to get a Father's Day present, who will? If the child goes empty-handed, who suffers? Yes, dad may be disappointed, but it is the child's wishes that are thwarted; it is the child who suffers. In situations where dad is remarried, the mother abdicates her role to the stepmother if she refuses to shop with her child. In this scenario the mother hurts herself and her relationship with her child.

If, on the other hand, the child's gift giving is supported, several positive things happen. The child perceives a lessening of tension between his divorced parents (even if it is not true). This perception makes the child more comfortable. The child benefits from the closeness that comes from parent and child shopping and talking. And most importantly, the child learns that being in a loving relationship involves responsibility. When you love someone, you give of yourself: You give your time and effort, and you buy loved ones gifts on certain occasions.

Thus, the gift-giving process that you share with your child benefits the child, teaches your child a sense of responsibility about loving relationships, and enhances your own relationship with your child. It only incidentally benefits your ex-spouse. Consequently, regardless of who has custody and who visits, dads should participate in shopping for Mother's Day, her birthday, Christmas, and any other occasion that is celebrated by gift giving. Similarly, mothers should participate with their children in shopping for Father's Day and all other gift-giving occasions.

Children receiving gifts from their parents can similarly stir up feelings of resentment, jealousy, and anger for parents. Hearing children go on and on about the terrific new 4X4 or the neat jeans can ruin the children's homecoming for a custodial mother. However, if these things make your child happy, there is no reason for resentment. If the gifts draw your children close to the other parent, it doesn't mean they are drawn away from you. Only if your resentment shows will the relationship with your child be damaged. The best response is to sit down and play with the 4X4 with your son and go through your daughter's closet to see what would look best with the new jeans. In this way you get into the gifts with your children, share their excitement and enthusiasm, and thereby enhance your relationship with them.

Often noncustodial parents watch gifts go home and never see them again. Too often it feels to such parents as though they're being taken advantage of; after all, they already provide child support. In response these parents sometimes give gifts that they will not allow the child to take home. Similarly, custodial parents may give gifts that they do not allow to be taken for visits. Remember, they are not gifts if they are not given free and clear. If you put restrictions on their use, you develop resentments in your children related to the gift-giving process and to their relationship with you. So don't do it. Let their possessions go freely back and forth. Your children will benefit and so will you. The only time this freedom should be curtailed is in situations where one parent, out of his or her own distorted values, confiscates the presents or destroys them. The only other situation in which gifts should not go home or go back and forth is when something is bought as a duplicate—for example, when a noncustodial parent buys a bicycle for a child to ride when he or she comes to visit, the child already having a bicycle at home.

Sometimes children in my office will tell me their mother or father is trying to "buy their love." This is not a concept children develop independently. Children love getting presents and they wouldn't deprecate the gift giver on their own. It is something they are taught by the resentful other parent. Rarely do parents really try to "buy" a child's love. When they do, the gifts are constant and elaborate. When the gifts don't achieve what they are intended to do—pull the child away from the other parent—

the gift giving stops. Overgenerous gift giving is seldom something with which to be concerned. It almost never works.

If children detect resentment and jealousy in both their parents, they will sometimes unwittingly play them off against each other. The result may be one parent trying to outdo the other with gifts. There are a lot of conscious and unconscious motives on the part of children for this behavior. Primarily, however, they experience a lack of support from both parents, feel caught in the middle of their continuing parental struggle, and in the absence of the emotional nurturing they need from their parents, they settle instead for "things": hence their manipulation. If your own gift giving to your children has increased and become more elaborate, perhaps even strapping you financially, it is likely you are caught in this struggle. Buy gifts that are age and occasion appropriate; buy gifts that do not stretch your budget. Your ex-spouse can't buy your children away from you. Remember that gift giving and receiving are loving exchanges between a parent and child. Share in the process and your children's enthusiasm and you will help foster appropriate growth and development; at the same time you will enhance the child-parent relationship.

Punishment: One Home to the Other

The behavior of children may vary from one parent's home to another. Some changes in behavior are to be expected with divorce. In addition, the tolerance and acceptance levels of parents change as they go through divorce. One parent may be more lenient with the children in an attempt to make sure they are not alienated. Another parent may become stricter in an attempt to bring some order to a life that feels chaotic and out of control. One child may become more well-behaved in an effort to please divorcing parents, while another child may become more disobedient, acting out fear and anger over the divorce. The possibilities are numerous and essentially unpredictable.

It is fairly common for divorcing parents to become more lenient or spoil their children in the initial stages of the divorce (announcement of the divorce until one year after the actual divorce). This is especially true for noncustodial parents. Mothers or fathers who feel they have lost their children and only see them every other weekend don't want to spend part of that precious little time punishing them. Even custodial parents, perhaps feeling insecure as single parents, are likely to be less strict after than before the divorce.

It is common for the custodial home to have stricter rules and more discipline than the other parent's home. Consequently, the custodial parent may frequently hear, "Why do I have to? I don't have to do that at dad's!" or "Dad lets us do that!" etc. Frustrated and perhaps even threatened by these comments, a mother may try to enforce discipline across homes. For example, if the child is grounded from watching television for some misbehavior, she may demand that the child not be allowed to watch TV in the father's home. Seldom will the other parent go along with this. Children and parents alike must learn that the homes are not equal. Punishment across homes does not work, is not fair to the children, is not fair to the parents, and should not be attempted. It is unfair for children and the noncustodial parent to be involved in disciplinary behavior that was instigated in the custodial home.

And finally, some important comments on discipline in general, regardless of whose home it is carried out in. Parents getting divorced is very frightening for children. Unfortunately, the adults are often so absorbed in their own change and worried about losing their children that their response is often to be lenient and overindulgent. This parental behavior actually frightens the children more and should be avoided. There is tremendous change for children when their parents divorce. A parent leaves; often homes are sold and schools changed. To have the rules change also (even though children might say they like it) just adds to the feeling that everything is out of control. Firm rules and guidelines are in the children's best interests. If the family's rules for behavior were appropriate prior to the divorce, they should be adhered to after the divorce. This sameness will actually be comforting to the children. It is something to be counted on.

Some comments about the severity of punishment for children: Children respond better to praise than punishment. Children respond better to punishment than nothing at all. When praise and positive reinforcement fail, or the behavior warrants punishment, the punishment should be swift and leave an impression but not be hurtful. Grounding a child from using the telephone for a week because that child hasn't cleaned his or her room interferes with a natural process in the child's life (the socializing process). A better punishment would be to have the child clean the room and the rest of the house before being allowed to go out on a weekend.

If possible, punishment should not be physical. Most children can be reasoned with—especially after the age of five. In addition, in a divorce situation, the use of physical punishment opens the parents to accusations of child abuse. The use of physical punishment can be turned against a parent by a manipulative child or a vindictive adult even when that punishment has been well intentioned. Consequently, physical punishment should be avoided.

Children Pitting Parents Against Each Other

Son: "Dad, can I go to the movies?"
Dad: "I don't know. What did mom say?"
Son: "I'll go ask her.
  "Mom, can I go the movies? Dad said it was okay if it was okay with you."
Mom: "Sure, if your father said it was okay."
Son: "Bye, Dad, I'm going to the movies. Mom said it was okay."

This kind of scenario is played out daily in thousands of happy homes. The parents perhaps are on a different level in the same house or perhaps in adjoining rooms, yet the child is capable of manipulating the situation to get what he wants. If it's that easy when it's a loving relationship and the parents are in the same house, imagine how easy it is when the parents don't like one another, live in separate places, and don't communicate often.

In the chaos of the divorce and the change in structure that follows, the children will take charge of whatever is available to them. Their security is of utmost importance, and they equate security with the attentiveness of the parents. The purpose is to be the center of attention. This attention may be received directly, as in gift giving, or it may be gained through the child's manipulation, which enables him or her to feel closely aligned with one parent and then the other. It is fairly common for children, feeling insecure in a divorce, to pit their parents against each other. They do this most often by highlighting behavior of one parent that they know will anger the other parent.

For example, a ten-year-old girl who lived with her mother complained that dad drank while she visited him and before he drove her home. Mother and father had been divorced in part because father drank too much. The daughter knew this and used it to her advantage to get closer to mom, who, she knew, would feel terrible her daughter had to be subjected to the same behavior she had been. Consequently the mother pulled the daughter closer. When the girl was with her father, she would tell him that her mother was a terrible rag, complaining about everything (a complaint father had had about his ex-wife for a long time before the divorce). Consequently he would pull her close. The adults refused to communicate about the problems because the child had successfully tapped into old resentments each harbored. Each parent actually identified with the child as if the two parents were still living together. Consequently, they blamed each other for mistreating their daughter. In this particular case the problems were not solved until petitions were filed in court and the judge referred the family to mediation. Once the manipulation was pointed out, the real problem could be focused on—the daughter's insecurity.

Lest you feel such manipulative children are simply nasty, mean little kids, let's look at the whole picture. Children who pit one parent against the other must feel a sense of desperation. Insecurity drives them to promote closeness in this way, but the unconscious, even conscious, guilt they have can be very painful. These are not happy, well-adjusted kids. The way for parents to help with this situation is to communicate openly in a nonaccusatory atmosphere. Only then will the manipulation of the child be undermined. Once this is accomplished, the reason for the manipulation must be dealt with—insecurity. Sometimes the source of the insecurity is obvious: both parents working, not enough time spent with the child, etc. Sometimes the reasons go deeper, and the child may need professional help.

Children's Reactions to Visits

During the initial stage of divorce—the separation through the end of the first year following the divorce—it is common to see a variety of reactions in children as they go from one home to the other. Tears, withdrawal, sullenness, anger, and silly, immature behavior are all common among children trying to adjust to shuttling between their parents' homes.

Preschool children are the quickest to adjust. Their reactions, if any, should be short-lived: two months and no longer. By the end of the first year following the divorce a preschooler will be hard pressed to remember what it was like living with both parents; going back and forth will seem very natural. If a preschooler is still having reactions after two months of regular visitation, then there is a problem in one of the parents' homes. The parents should talk about the reactions, and if the problem and its solution does not emerge from these discussions, then professional help should be sought.

The most common reaction of school-age children during visits is tentativeness: hesitancy to emotionally let themselves go and be comfortable. Their facial expressions will appear guarded, as if they were being introduced to a new person. They may actually have to be invited to play with things or turn on the television. An excessive exuberance may follow in which they will test the limits of the rules of the home. These reactions occur because children are not used to seeing their parents in new contexts. Children seem to need a brief period of feeling the situation out before they let themselves go.

Furthermore, the separation that requires children to see their parents in new places is usually preceded by some arguments. Often the arguments continue throughout the early stages of the divorce. The children, uncertain of the parents' moods following arguments, approach cautiously. Actually this reaction is very commonplace in all homes. Even in an intact family, if parents argue children are likely to approach them cautiously until they are confident they will be well received. We simply recognize this caution more in separation and divorce because we are anticipating with some joy the visit or return of our children and are dismayed by their hesitancy. Once the children are assured we are accepting them, their exuberance returns—often to the extreme, as they test the limits of the new situation.

The hesitancy-exuberance reaction will occur both as children go from the custodial home to the visited home and as they go from the visited home back to the custodial home. When the parental separation-divorce is new, the hesitancy part of the reaction may last longer (perhaps for an entire visit) or for the balance of the day when children return to the custodial home. As the children become more comfortable, the hesitancy part of the reaction will shorten; then the exuberance will shorten. Eventually both should disappear.

When the children visit, the reason for the reaction is concern over their acceptance by the parent that has left home. When the children return home, the reason for their reaction is concern over whether they're still loved after visiting the other parent. Assurance of your love combined with firm limit-setting on behavior goes a long way in making children in this situation more comfortable.

Parents are often disturbed by the initial hesitancy and may wonder if the children have been turned against them by the other parent. Assurance of love will help the children through their reactions and calm parental fears.

Occasionally one parent will attempt to turn a child against the other parent. In this situation the hesitancy-exuberance reaction will not be witnessed. What will be demonstrated is either total withdrawal and sullenness or outright anger and hostility. These behaviors are often followed by pleasant periods in which the parent and child get along; then the reactive behavior returns prior to the end of the visit. Obviously other problems can create withdrawal or hostile behavior in your child. Don't automatically assume that a child exhibiting this behavior has been turned against you. However, if a parent has attempted to do that, withdrawal or hostile behavior will be the reaction.

Another common reaction to early visits may be tears and/or reluctance: to visit the noncustodial parent or to go home after the visit is over. This reaction is nothing more than a demonstration of the child's difficulty separating from a parent to whom the child is attached. Reassurance about when the child will see that parent again and that the parent will also miss the child should be sufficient to help the child through the reaction. If the reaction is especially strong, the parents might consider temporarily suspending overnight visits until the child gets used to the transitions. However, this should be a last resort. Most children will stop crying as soon as they are out of the parent's sight. Unfortunately, many parents unconsciously promote such behavior (see the next section of this chapter, "Parents' Reactions to Visits"), and this only serves to make the reaction last longer.

Remember, reactions to visits at the beginning of divorce and the initiation of visitation are common and normal. However, reactions to visits later on should be viewed as a warning sign that your child is disturbed about something. Parents' put-downs of each other, sibling or stepsibling problems, children's attempts to pit parents against each other, stepparent problems, and severe insecurity can all produce reactions pre- and postvisitation. If you can't discover the problem from conversation with your son or daughter, talk to your ex-spouse. If this doesn't bring about a solution and the reaction is continuing, take your child for some professional help—preferably from someone who is accustomed to seeing children of divorce.

Parents' Reactions to Visits

During the initial stages of separation and divorce, parents, like children, go through a period of adjustment characterized by feelings of insecurity. If the children know who initiated the divorce, that parent may worry about the children's anger in response to their action. The noncustodial parent may worry that the children will have a negative reaction to his or her not being around every day. The custodial parent may be concerned about the children's reactions because being a single parent entails more responsibility, which frequently means more time spent away from them.

Consequently, when the first hesitancy reaction (see previous section) takes place before or after visitation, many parents feel it is their due. They feel guilty about what has happened to their children and see this as the price they must pay. The reality is that the children are hesitant as a result of their own insecurity. Another reaction parents sometimes have is anger. They're angry that their children are not responding to them and angry at their ex-spouse, whom they often see as responsible for this behavior. Anger is the worst response for children already anxious about their parents' acceptance of them. Love and reassurance will eventually get the children out of their hesitancy, while anger will only deepen it. If the anger is directed at the other parent, it will serve to alienate the children even further as they emotionally draw closer to the attacked parent.

Of all the children's reactions, the most difficult for a parent to deal with is tears and/or reluctance to go—to go on visits or to go home after visits. Remember, this reaction is only serious if it comes after the initial stages of divorce or if, in the beginning stages, it doesn't subside after proper parental response. Then it may be an indication of a problem in the custodial or visited home. Frequently, however, it is difficult to determine if there is a real problem because parents often unconsciously promote this behavior.

When a child cries or is reluctant to visit or go home, a parent feels concern, but also often some quiet satisfaction from the thought that the child prefers him or her to the ex-spouse. If the tears are not in response to a real problem, they will disappear with reassurance of parental love. If, however, a parent is oversolicitous of the child's feelings, these feelings are likely to continue (often to the parent's unconscious delight). Sometimes custodial parents will unwittingly or manipulatively schedule exciting events while a child is visiting, thereby facilitating this tearful reaction. Trips to grandma's or the amusement park should be avoided when the child is away and saved for times when the child is available to participate in this activity.

Parents' reactions to visits are not always reactions to the children's moods. Sometimes they are reactions to the reality of divorce that come crashing home before, during, and after children's visits. Even marital partners who want to be away from each other are struck by the loneliness of being separated not only from that spouse but from the children as well. Children have a way of filling space with sound, motion, and mass that is not comparable to anything or anyone else. Consequently, their absence is remarkably noticeable, especially for most mothers. No matter what the custody arrangement, mothers are in the vast majority of cases more closely bonded to their children than are fathers in our society. When the children leave for the first few visits, it is often very difficult for them. Tears and weekends of depression are common. It is a good idea to fill weekends when the children are away with activities with friends and responsibilities such as laundry, cleaning, and grocery shopping.

Another reaction, experienced equally by mothers and fathers, is anger. Unlike the anger discussed earlier, this anger is not related to your children. However, sometimes the anger is expressed at the children, sometimes at the ex-spouse; often it is not directed at anyone in particular. This anger in reality has to do with the divorce itself, feelings about the marriage, feelings about the ex-marital partner, and frustration with yourself. It gets stirred up when children go visiting or return home because these moments bring the reality of divorce into sharp focus. Anger with your children before, during, and after visits is understandable but is an immature response and should be brought under control. This reaction and others, like the children's reactions, will be short-lived. If, however, your reactions do not stop after several months, you should seek professional help. It is likely that the separation from the children is setting off a deeper pain associated with a sense of abandonment.

Parent-Parent Put-downs

During the initial stages of divorce and frequently long after the divorce has actually taken place, parents will disagree, argue, and fight. The comments from the section titled "Blame for the Divorce," in Chapter 2, are applicable here. Don't put down the child's other parent to the child or in conversation with another person in your child's presence. Don't allow your family and friends to put down your ex to your child or in your child's presence. Regardless of how often I emphasize this to parents and explain the detrimental effects put-downs have on the child and the child-parent relationship, I still have kids tell me, "I was watching TV and mom was in the kitchen on the phone telling Aunt Sue that daddy . . . ".

There are essentially three reasons for parent-parent put-downs: (1) They may be leftover interactions from the marriage or new anger over postdecree interactions, (2) they may stem from the fear of losing the children, and (3) they may be defenses against put-downs initiated by the ex-spouse.

Starting with the last reason first, don't compound the trouble your ex-spouse has started by defensively putting him or her down to your child. If the child says, "Daddy, mommy says I can't get a new bike 'cause you don't give her enough money," mom obviously feels guilty over not being able to provide something she'd like to for her child and has dealt with the guilt by blaming dad. Dad can give it back to her, using his child as the vehicle— as in: "If your mother would do what she is supposed to with the money I give her, there would be plenty to buy you a bike"—or he can defuse the situation by saying something like, "When moms and dads live in different places, it costs a lot more, and sometimes there isn't enough money for all the things we want." If mom had better control of her anger and guilt she could have originally said this to the child when questioned about the bike. Trading put-downs puts children in the middle of a war between two people they love. The children lose and neither one of the parents win.

Fear of losing the children to the other parent is another reason for such put-downs. As explained earlier, in divorce everything is divided up except the children; the children are shared. No one parent has exclusive ownership of them or their loyalties. Unfortunately, your insecurity can get stirred up when you hear your child talk lovingly about your ex-spouse. You may find yourself countering these glowing comments with negative remarks in some vain attempt to hold the child close. Depending on the viciousness of the remarks, you may in fact pull your child close and negate some of the intimacy with the other parent. However, the child will eventually see through this, become angry at you for interfering with his or her relationship with the other parent, and pull away from you. There may be short-term gains in parental put-downs; but there is almost always long-term loss. And it always causes emotional strain and problems for the children.

The last reason for such put-downs, and perhaps the most common one, is ex-partners still being angry with each other over marital issues or postdivorce issues such as money, possessions, time spent with children, etc. It would be naive to suggest that you not fight with your ex-spouse. It is not naive, or inappropriate, to implore you not to put your children in the middle, or worse, use them as vehicles for your anger: "Tell your father if he can't be here at 5 o'clock to pick you up he can forget it altogether." Put-downs of the other parent create problems enough for children—divide loyalties, force choices, and cause emotional conflict. It is much worse to force a child to be the vehicle for that anger.

In situations where children are in some jeopardy, as with an alcoholic or abusive parent, and they need to be protected, re-stricted visitations and other controls can be utilized without re-sorting to parent-parent put-downs.

Child-Parent Put-downs

Child-parent put-downs are almost always manipulative. "Mom, dad grounded me all day. It was terrible. I had to spend all day in my room, I couldn't watch TV, I didn't even get lunch." Mom calls dad, furious, only to find out that the child was grounded for an hour, chose to spend the better part of the day in her room, and wasn't hungry when lunch was offered. "Dad, it's terrible. I'm just a maid there. Mom makes me clean my room and the rest of the house too. I even have to do the toilet." Dad's concerned call reveals that, indeed, his child is responsible for keeping her room clean. However, cleaning the rest of the house only refers to picking up after herself and not leaving her clothes and books scattered about. And the toilet? Yes, she's doing the toilet and the rest of the bathroom once a week for an extra $5 allowance.

So why do kids do this? Basically there are two reasons. The first is for sympathetic attention. Children are aware of the lack of communication and trust between divorced parents. Children who get involved in child-parent put-downs (not all children of divorce do this) take advantage of this lack of communication and trust to get sympathy from the other parent. The motivation for the behavior is insecurity. It is not uncommon for a child to be putting down each parent to the other simultaneously. Obviously the way to combat this is to (1) recognize children's and teenagers' propensity for exaggeration, and (2) reestablish a sense of trust in your ex-spouse (at least where it involves the children) and communicate more.

The second reason for such behavior is the child's identification with one parent and the need to attach more closely to that parent, expressed by putting down the other parent. This only happens when the child is exposed to repeated parent-parent put-downs. Again, the reason for the behavior is insecurity. Often the child enjoys the time spent with the put-down parent and no negatives can be seen in the relationship. If the parent the child needs to be closer to has an intense hatred of the ex-spouse, however, there is a possibility that the child will turn against the put-down parent. As explained in the previous section, this is detrimental to everyone, but especially to the children involved.

Of concern to the parents, of course, in either of the above situations is the truth or legitimacy of what the child is saying. What if we take the comments lightly and believe they are only child-parent put-downs when in fact there is abuse or negligence in one of the homes and the child is trying to communicate this? All put-downs must be listened to, questioned, and their validity challenged; for example, "That's a serious thing to say about dad. Are you sure you're not just upset with him?" If the child stands behind the put-down, the other parent must be contacted, but with a tone of concern, not accusations. Often truth lies somewhere between what the child says and what the other parent says. The real test of whether it's a child-parent put-down or a legitimate reporting of some abuse is whether it's repeated. If so, it needs to be taken seriously, and professional, even legal help sought in dealing with the situation.

Telephone Calls

Some noncustodial parents and their children talk on the phone every day; some almost never call between visits. Neither way is right or wrong; neither is even that much of an extreme. (An extreme is many calls a day; an extreme is no visits.) However, parents who have telephone contact with their children are clearly going to have a closer relationship with their children than parents who don't.

Noncustodial parents should call their children regularly—I recommend every other day, although there is nothing wrong with slightly more or slightly less. The calls do not have to be lengthy. Most will probably be under five minutes. Don't stand on ceremony with your children. They are not imbued with adult social etiquette and, even if they were, childhood and adolescence is too selfish a period for them to follow it—so don't wait for them to call. You'll be disappointed. Noncustodial parents will make 80 percent of all phone calls. The purpose of the contact is to reassure them that you love them and that they are not forgotten.

Sometimes phone calls can be a disturbance in custodial homes. If you are a noncustodial parent you must be aware that every time you call you are entering the custodial home, almost like a guest. When you are sensitive to that, you won't call too late or at dinnertime, and you'll be polite to whomever answers the phone. Remember, you are in no position for a power struggle. Without the custodial parent's cooperation you won't find phone access to your child easy.

Custodial parents should support their children's phone contact with their other parent. All this means is, do not interfere with the contact and be polite if you happen to answer the phone. Give privacy to the child if it's asked.

For the most part, custodial parents do not need to make calls to their children when the children are visiting. With typical visitation (every other weekend), custodial parents are only away from their children for one full day. They see them on Friday before they leave and on Sunday when they return; Saturday is the only day they have no contact. Consequently it is unnecessary, unless in an emergency or for very important news, to interrupt visitation with phone calls. The only exception to this rule is when visitation is first starting. The loneliness for the first few weekends will be difficult for children to handle, and a couple of brief phone calls would be helpful.

On the other hand, children should be supported if they choose to call the custodial home during visitation. Young children especially may want to say good night to the custodial parent who normally tucks them into bed. Remember, for custodial and noncustodial parents alike, supporting a telephone relationship that is desired by the child only endears the child to you. You lose nothing, and you support the child's sense of well-being.

Sleeping with Children

Don't sleep with your children. Don't sleep with them regardless of their age, sex, or whether you are the custodial or noncustodial parent.

Often parents will say, "Johnny was scared by the storm and climbed in bed with me," or "Sally had a nightmare and was afraid to sleep alone." Unfortunately, it is different for a small child, frightened by the boogeyman, to climb in bed between both parents than for the child to get in bed with a single parent. Unconsciously it is different for the child, and it is different for the parent and suspicious in the eyes of our society. Much could be written here about Oedipal issues, sexual identity, curiosity, attachment and bonding, and conflict and guilt in this area. However, to be brief, all indicators are that it is not beneficial for the child to sleep with the single parent. Parents and children can have wonderfully close and intimate relationships and can feel attached and bonded, intimate and loved, without sleeping together.

I am not referring to the child who bounces into bed at 8 o'clock on a Sunday morning to watch cartoons while mom or dad is reading the newspaper. As long as both are dressed, this is acceptble and enjoyable. I am only speaking of situations in which parents regularly sleep with their children—this is unacceptable. It can ultimately create emotional problems for your child and, in a society that has became very sensitive to issues of child sexual abuse, can result in an accusation of misconduct for the parent.

So, what if the child, frightened by nightmares or a storm, wakes you up and asks to get into bed? What the child is really asking for is to feel safe and secure. Being in bed alone didn't feel secure. The parent should walk the child back to bed, tuck the child in, and remain there until the child falls back asleep or at least until it is obvious that the child is comfortable again.

Too Many Activities

Children of divorce can be overwhelmed by too many activities more easily than children from intact nuclear families. Sometimes children are in a different organized sport each season, take music lessons, belong to Scouts, and go to Sunday school. In an effort to have children well-rounded, parents can overdo it. Children need time to imagine, reflect, and create without structured activities. And, importantly, children need time to deal with their emotions—alone as well as in conversation with peers and parents. Too many activities will rob them of this kind of time. This is especially true for children of divorce.

The most important activity for children of divorce is visitation—being with the other parent. Custodial parents often have a tendency to overschedule their children. There are three reasons for this. The reasons may be conscious or subconscious. First, most custodial parents work, and when home, they have a myriad of household responsibilities. When they're done, they're tired, and feel guilty that they don't have more of themselves to give to their children. The activities help ease their guilt. Second, activities can provide baby-sitting in addition to teaching skills and entertaining. Third, activities interfere with visitation.

It is nearly impossible to have children in activities and never have a conflict between the activities and visitation. Simply because they overlap does not mean that they are purposely being used to interfere with visitation. However, when activities continually interfere with visitation everyone needs to look at the motivation for and the purpose of the activities. Everyone gets hurt in this situation. The custodial parent's motives are challenged, the noncustodial parent's desire to be with the children is thwarted, and the children are torn between things they like to do and adults they want to be with; if they do one thing they may be disappointed, and if they do the other they may feel guilty.

Most activities can be scheduled during nonvisitation times. Scouting is usually after school. Music lessons, art classes, dance lessons, and most other classes can similarly be scheduled after school. Organized sports, however, are often on weekends. If children have the talent and interest then they should be encouraged to participate. All sports, however, are seasonal. With some slight alterations—missing a week here and there of the activity, missing a week here or there of visitation, combining these two with the noncustodial parent coming to some of the events—the season can be gotten through with a minimal amount of disruption to visitation. It's when the lessons are scheduled on weekends and the child is encouraged to participate in one sport after the other throughout the year that activities become excessive and do violence to the visitation process.

If it appears that too many activities are being scheduled, talk to your ex-spouse about your concerns. If this is not possible or your ex-spouse is not responsive, seek mediation. If cooperation is still lacking, contact your attorney. Visitation needs to be a priority. If it is being interfered with and manipulated, everyone will be left with feelings of bitterness, resentment, and guilt. Overscheduling activities is not in the best interests of the children.

Going to the Kids' Activities

School plays, open houses, recitals, awards dinners, talent shows, and various sports are a few of the events that almost all children participate in. All of these activities are opportunities for children to be the focus of attention and to receive acknowledgment for their accomplishments. Both parents should be in attendance if possible, regardless of which parent's home the child is in when the activity takes place.

Many ex-couples have great difficulty being in the same room together. If that's the case, then some communication prior to the event is appropriate to determine which of the parents will attend. For the noncustodial parent, responsibility does not start and stop with visitation. Extending yourself to be at your child's recital, even though it is not "your" day, will be a thrill to your child and help draw both of you close.

Without question, one of the places divorce is experienced as a hardship for children is in the area of activities. It is good for children to be in extracurricular activities. It is harmful if the activities are excessive or too often at the expense of visitation. While visitation is definitely the priority, rigid adherence to this rule can sometimes frustrate and anger children. Flexibility with this rule will be appreciated by your children. However, permissively allowing activities to interfere will frustrate the parent. Finding a balance is critical.

On occasion activities will take place on days or over weekends that the children are scheduled to be with the noncustodial parent. When this happens, noncustodial parents sometimes feel their time has been intruded upon. Unless these occasions are excessive (see previous section), the child is simply living a normal, balanced life. Visitation is clearly a top priority, but it should not be had at the expense of important activities or events. If it is, resentment will develop. If, however, the child feels that the noncustodial parent is willing to go out of the way to take the child to an important activity, then the child will be more inclined to give up some activities for visitation.

If a child has been invited to the birthday party of a favorite friend on the Friday night of visitation, make arrangements to pick up the child on Saturday morning. If a child is to play in a soccer game on the Saturday of visitation, take the child for the weekend but make sure the child gets to the soccer game. Responding in this manner to these relatively slight inconveniences will only solidify your relationship with your child and will help the child lead a relatively normal life. Part of this normal life is to play with friends on weekends. Often it is frustrating for children of divorce and their friends to say good-bye every other weekend. Be sensitive to this and occasionally invite your kids to bring a friend for the weekend. They may or may not take you up on the offer, but regardless, the offer and its availability will take some of the sting out of the bimonthly good-byes.

Stepparents

Throughout their development, children form many different levels of attachment to adults. Teachers, coaches, aunts and uncles, grandparents, doctors, and parents are some of the people with whom these attachments may form. None of these relationships are any more intense, fraught with potential conflict, potentially loving, and emotional as the relationship between a child and a stepparent.

In our society, the concept of stepparent is largely negative. Wicked stepmother and lecherous stepfather are phrases that describe a child-adult relationship which is mean, abusive, and hurtful. Even our fairy tales foster this concept—"Cinderella" is a prime example. Moreover, many child-stepparent relationships *are* negative, thereby perpetuating these attitudes. However, many of these relationships are positive and loving. With some understanding of children of divorce and some simple rules of behavior, most of these relationships can be positive. If you are a divorced parent worried about your children's adjustment to a potential stepparent, remember, you also may be a stepparent some day.

Preschool children treated with sensitivity and kindness quickly form positive attachments. They are less aware of parental jealousies and the sense of exclusiveness in parent-child relationships than are older children. Consequently their attachments are more rapid and more likely to be based solely on elements of that particular child-parent relationship. Older children will proceed more cautiously. Stepparent-child relationships will be positive if

1. both natural parents support the stepparent's involvement with the children
2. the stepparent is kind
3. the stepparent is fair
4. the stepparent shows a genuine interest in the child's activities

5. the stepparent spends some individual time with the child
6. the child doesn't feel that the stepparent has interfered with the relationship with the natural parent
7. there is unity of purpose between the stepparent and the natural parent

Most of these points are self-explanatory, yet some are worth more discussion. Without the support of both natural parents, stepparenting ranges from difficult to impossible. It is important for divorced parents to realize that, just as the love a child has for one parent doesn't diminish the child's love for the other, the attachment a child forms with a stepparent doesn't diminish the attachment to the natural parent. When a stepparent comes on the scene, parental jealousy is natural. However, to act on this jealousy and attempt to interfere with the child-stepparent involvement is immature and ultimately hurtful to your child. The more positive role models children have in their lives the better. Avoid parent-parent put-downs in which the stepparents are involved the same way you avoid the parent-parent put-downs regarding your ex-spouse.

If you become a stepparent yourself, remember the importance of fairness and the appearance of impartiality. Children are extremely sensitive to these issues. If your discipline of a natural child and a stepchild is unequal and unfair, it will be quickly noted. Resentments will soon develop, and they are difficult to counteract. No one is suggesting that you love your stepchild like your own, although such love may develop as the years go by. It is strongly suggested, however, that you appear fair to all the children in the family.

Sometimes a child will react negatively to a stepparent or a prospective stepparent despite the adult's fairness and open fondness for the child. After the trauma of divorce is survived, the nature of the child's relationship with the parents changes. It is no longer necessary to say "Excuse me" to interrupt the parents' conversation or follow behind as they walk hand in hand. After divorce these situations no longer exist. But as the parents form new adult relationships, the child will have to contend with them. The response may be comfort in the parent's happiness and a sense of family, or frustration if the stepparent is seen as a competitor for the natural parent's affection and attention. If the child feels jealous, then some time should be given to the child by the natural parent, yet it should be made clear that this new family, including the stepparent, will now be the order of the day. The child is especially vulnerable to these feelings when the stepparent is married to the noncustodial parent. The child doesn't see this parent as often as the custodial parent and is therefore more likely to experience feelings of jealousy if the stepparent is always part of the picture.

If you are contemplating remarriage, make sure your prospective marital partner loves kids. Raising children can be a demanding task under the best of circumstances, and a blended family is not the best of circumstances. Both adults must be committed not only to each other, but, as a primary goal in their relationship, committed to the responsibilities of child-raising and seeing the children through adolescence and into their adult lives. If one of the partners does not like children or doesn't share in this commitment, then more likely than not the two of them will argue and fight about the children and run the risk of eventually destroying their own relationship.

Stepsiblings

Stepbrothers and stepsisters come in three varieties—those who live in the same homes as the natural children, those who visit the home where the natural children live, and those who live with the noncustodial parent and are there when the natural children visit. Stepsiblings have the potential for being wonderful friends—even closer than natural brothers and sisters. More likely than not, however, there will be all the jealousies and resentments common among natural siblings, magnified by the fact that the stepsiblings are not related and further complicated by stepparent involvement.

The key to the children's adjustment is with the parents. In the truly blended family—two divorced parents marrying, both with custody of children—the adults must take firm control in order to

make it feel like a family. Personal possessions are often the battleground where the war of words and emotions is fought. "That's
my TV and I'll watch what I want to" or "This is my home—don't
tell me what to do" or "My mom said I could" are common examples of the power moves kids will make as they attempt to find
their place in the new family.

Insecurity motivates this behavior. In time all the children
should find a slot for themselves, feel loved, and have a sense of
belonging. Until then, however, left unstructured, they will
scratch and claw for their place of comfort. When the possessive-
ness begins to disappear in their conversations, you can feel confident that the blending is beginning to take place.

The blending will be facilitated if you

1. establish one set of rules for all children
2. have responsibilities for all children—some the same (e.g.,
   homework) and some different (garbage, dishes, yard-
   work, etc.)
3. encourage and promote sharing of possessions through
   acknowledgment and praise
4. encourage time spent alone with each parent for each
   child
5. encourage time spent as a family
6. don't let your child pit you against your stepchild
7. have adult time to talk about what's going on in the
   family

Remember, even in the best of intact families, siblings quarrel
and bicker. Some of this is just normal, and you can't expect to
put out every fire that starts. However, if the expectation in the
family is that "we are all one family and we're going to get along,"
the children themselves will begin to solve their own differences.
The attitudes start with the parents' unity of purpose. The task
of blending a family is difficult. The period of adjustment is any-
where between six months and a year.

Sometimes it's easier to blend families than it is to deal with
the stepsibling issues when children are visitors, as when children visit on weekends a parent who is remarried to someone who

has custody of his or her own children. It is difficult to blend a family for two or three days every other weekend and then regain the sense of family that existed before the visit. The children who live in the house feel their space and sense of place is violated with these visits, while the children who visit feel like outsiders in their parent's home. It is not likely these feelings will change to any great degree, for the visiting children are never in the home long enough to work out the problems. However, if the parents are sensitive and encourage both sets of kids to talk about their feelings (without repercussions for how they feel), then the feelings are less likely to be acted out in a destructive way during visitation.

It will be especially difficult for a parent to listen to a stepchild talk negatively about the parent's natural child. If, however, both parents are in on the conversation, the stepchild's natural parent can be supportive of the other child so that it doesn't appear that parents are always lined up on the side of their own children. Handled with this kind of sensitivity, the natural jealousies and resentments among stepsiblings can be held to a minimum.

Flexibility in Visitation

All too often parents want to follow the provisions of the divorce decree rigidly with regard to visitation. It is as if they think losing an hour here or there means they will lose their children, or perhaps the thought is, "She got the house and kids, so I'm going to make sure I get everything else that's coming to me." Regardless of the motivation, such rigidity is not in the children's best interests, nor will it serve to enhance child-parent relationships. On the other hand, a reliable structure of visitation is necessary for children and parents to count on. There is an in-between.

If a parent with visitation rights is entitled to parts of ten days a month with the children (every other weekend and one night a week), then over a year's time this amount of time should be approximated. A 15 percent variation on either side is acceptable. In other words, if there are 120 days of visitation each year (not counting holidays and vacation), then visitation of somewhere between 102 and 138 days is acceptable to maintain good contact between parent and child.

How this flexibility is negotiated, however, is not always easy. Business, social, and family commitments on the part of both parents, combined with the activities and social commitments of the children, all play an important role. Remember, visitation is the priority, and to interfere with visitation, an event should be important. The birthday party of a special friend may not seem important to a parent who hasn't seen his or her child in a week, but it is nevertheless important to the child. Many of these decisions need to be made from the child's perspective. Of course, the other side of this is that children need to make sacrifices and learn about doing things for others. Consequently, grandma's seventieth birthday party has priority over a baseball game.

When noncustodial parents lose visitation time, either because of the children's needs, the needs of the custodial home, or the commitments of the noncustodial parent, some attempt should be made to make up this time. If that is not easily accomplished, however, then the time should simply remain lost until some extra time can be arranged down the road. Too often parents get hung up on the actual hours spent. Five or ten hours here or there are not worth World War III with the ex-spouse. That's the reason for the 15 percent leeway per calendar year. When your children are twenty-five years old, they won't remember whether they were with you 105 days a year or 125 days a year. What they will remember are the feelings of closeness or distance and the special occasions or the sense of being forced to visit only to watch TV when they wanted to be with their friends.

As children get into their teenage years, their needs begin changing dramatically as they go through the transition between childhood and adulthood on physical, emotional, and intellectual levels. Their activities change, as does their need for emotional input from their parents. Changes in visitation will be necessary. To strictly adhere to the visitation schedule set up when the children were eight or ten now that they are fourteen or sixteen would not be in their best interests. This will be discussed fully in the section in the next chapter called "Changing Needs of Children."

Communication Issues

The first section of this chapter discussed how straightforward the custody/visitation system can be. Indeed, there are many divorced couples with children who have very little communication, and what they do have is brief and to the point. The system works well. The children know and understand the structure, and relatively smooth transitions take place from one home to the other and from one stage of child development to the other. But for many couples these transitions are difficult, frequently resulting in bitter disagreements and occasionally necessitating trips to the courtroom for solutions.

Divorce seldom occurs without bitterness and resentment. Divorce also breeds insecurity, in adults as well as children. Remaining sensitive to these issues will serve everyone well. If you are running late when the kids are due home from visitation, don't allow your ex-spouse to sit worrying by the front door. It will scare your ex-spouse, arouse anger, and provoke a retaliatory response. A thirty-second call to say you'll be an hour late and not to worry will save everyone—including you—a lot of grief. Similarly, don't disappoint your children. If you told them you'd pick them up at 5 o'clock, be there at 5. If you can't, call. You've never seen dejection and disappointment until you've watched a child sit by a window waiting for a car that never comes. You can almost see the minutes go by in the increasing pain etched in the child's eyes. If a child has gotten sick and visitation must be canceled, don't let the other parent find out when he or she comes to pick up the kids. Call in advance. If any plans for visitation need to be changed, regardless of who's responsible for the change, communicate this as far in advance as possible.

Divorce, and the adjustment to it, can make everyone a little leery about change. Therefore, if any major changes are going to take place, inform and communicate well in advance so that everyone has time to adjust. For example, a change in residence requires a visit to the new home to show the children how far it is from other important things like friends and the other parent. Some adjustment time is necessary. This would not be a pleasant surprise, and as a parent you would be disappointed by their less than enthusiastic response if you sprung it on the children. The same holds true for a remarriage. While it will be an exciting, joyous occasion in your life, it means a significant adjustment on the part of your children and ex-spouse. Let them know well in advance.

And finally, use your community in this inform-and-communicate process. Your children will benefit. When the divorce process begins and the children have been told, tell the other significant people in their lives—their teachers, troop leaders, coaches, etc.—so that they will understand your children's behavior and can help deal with the children's reactions.

Chapter 4

Changing Custody and Visitation

Custody Is Not Forever

Remember, custody is not ownership. Too many people going through divorce look at the children as one more thing a couple divides in their settlement. While our children belong to us, they are not our possessions like the stereo or the television. They have rights and laws to protect them. We can do what we want with the stereo, but we cannot do what we want with our children. Indeed, when we are divorced, there are even more rules and laws that govern the treatment of the chidren. Where they must be on certain holidays, particular weekends, and for certain other periods of time is all dictated by court order.

As the years go by, more and more people get involved in influencing the lives and development of the children: There is the other parent, the court, eventually perhaps a stepmother, a stepfather, and stepchildren, as well as half-brothers and half-sisters, in addition to the elements that have an impact on all children—school, neighborhood, etc. Combine these factors with children's changing needs as they grow—peer involvement, independence (e.g., having a job), love relationships—and we soon recognize that our own role as parent evolves from omnipresent protector and nurturer to part-time counselor and guide.

The upshot of all this is that custody is nothing more than parenthood—custody is simply a legal term—and parenthood has many changing faces as children grow. Custody denotes legal responsibility. Too often it seems to divorcing parents that custody is somehow more than parenthood; something more powerful, more controlling. It isn't. Divorced parenthood is more difficult and more complicated, but it is still nothing more than parenthood.

When we live with our spouse we share varied responsibilities of parenthood—no one person has to do it all. Divorce brings more individual responsibility, but we still don't have to do it all. A custodial mother can't do all the practical things necessary for her children and go to the ball games, teach them to sew and drive nails, fix their bikes, and take them to music lessons, any more than a custodial father could fulfill all his daily responsibilities and teach his children manners, take them camping or fishing, teach them to cook, and build models with them. If parenthood has many faces and custody is nothing more than parenthood, then custody is really "joint" regardless of what the court says. This is only true, however, if both parents remain invested in their children's development. And finally, as the phases of childhood progress, the nature of parenting responsibilities changes until at last parenting denotes a kind of loving relationship with few responsibilities. When a child reaches eighteen, custody ends. The common changes in custody and visitation over time are the subject of the rest of the sections in this chapter.

Changing Needs of Children

It is obvious to all of us that the needs of a two-year-old are different from the needs of a seven-year-old, and that the needs of a seven-year-old are different from the needs of a fifteen-year-old. It is also true, but perhaps less obvious, that the needs of boys are sometimes different from the needs of girls—especially for school-age children and teenagers. And, not as apparent, there are often differences between the needs of only children and children with siblings; frequently there are differences between first-, second-, and third-born children. When you combine the age variations, gender differences, and birth order considerations, the needs of children and how they change can be extremely intricate and complex.

We are sensitive to many of these changes as our children grow. Often a mother will say to her husband, "You know, you've been working long hours lately and Billy misses spending some time with you. Why don't the two of you go fishing on Sunday." Or a father might say to his wife, "I noticed Jenny has started sucking her thumb again. I think she's jealous of the baby. Maybe this weekend I can watch the baby and you guys can do something on your own." Picking up the slack and tuning in to each other's needs and the needs of the children is part of what marriage and parenthood is all about. Partners who know each other's strengths as parents can use them to help their kids grow.

Unfortunately with divorce, and the bitterness and resentment that tend to accompany it, the parental strengths of our ex-partners are often seen as a threat that could jeopardize our children's attachment to us or our having custody. It is an unusually secure parent who can hand a child over to the other parent and say, "You do this better than I do, and he needs more of what you have to offer." Yet this is exactly what all children of divorce need—two parents with different parental and personality strengths and talents, two parents to interact with and be nurtured by, depending on the children's varying needs.

All too often during custody negotiations, a wife will say, "All of a sudden he's Superdad, playing with the kids and spending time with them. When they were babies, he couldn't be bothered. He never gave them a bath or changed a diaper." The implication or explicit comment that follows is that he really doesn't care about the kids or is being vindictive. Similarly, the husband might say, "Now that she works and goes to school, the kids never see her anymore. I have to do it all." The implication is that she no longer cares about the children.

It is true that some few men will vindictively try to pull their children away from the mother, and some few women are so selfish as to forego their parental responsibilities in pursuit of their own needs. However, most women in this situation are merely taking advantage of the availability of an ex-spouse to further their education or career and provide more income for their family. And more men in the above situation simply relate better to children and adolescents than they do to infants and therefore have more to do with their kids as they grow and mature. The resentments engendered by divorce, or fear of losing the children, are what make these situations look negative.

Which parent is a better caretaker, providing for meals, clean clothes, clean environment, proper rest, and medical care? Which parent is a better communicator, eliciting conversation about thoughts and feelings, friends and family? Which parent is a good teacher, helping the child to run and play, ride a bike and throw a ball? Which parent promotes the activities of going to museums, zoos, and grandma's house? Which parent is best at helping the child work out personal problems? Which parent patiently helps with homework? Which parent promotes a religious education? Which parent provides a role model for sexual identity? Which parent comfortably answers questions about sexuality? These questions and their answers will have changing weight and significance as the children grow. (By no means are the above questions meant to be all-inclusive. They are examples.) A six-year-old child needs a lot of love and nurturing and a sense of protection and caretaking from his or her parents. That same child at fifteen needs a role model, a good communicator to discuss problems with and plan a future, someone who supports education and with whom they can talk about girlfriends and boyfriends. Sometimes all of these abilities are embodied in one parent, and sometimes various needs are better met by different parents.

The biggest shifts in children's needs will be around pre-puberty, puberty, and early adolescence. Depending on the individual child's rate of maturing, both physical and emotional, these shifts will take place between the ages of ten and sixteen. It is often during these years that there will be changes in visitation (increasing or decreasing) and even changes in physical custody with various degrees of visitation for the former custodial parent. Sometimes these shifts are brought about by other factors, like a job change on the part of a parent or the presence of a step-parent, but often they happen because of the changing needs of the children and the different abilities of the parents to meet these developmental needs.

Parents Stopping Visitation

Twenty years ago it was not uncommon for noncustodial parents to disappear, stopping visitation and essentially walking out of their children's lives. Especially if the children were preschoolers, such parents often felt that it would be less of a hassle to stop visiting than to continue to deal with uncooperative ex-spouses. Since the majority of divorced people marry again within five years of their divorce, the children would probably have a stepparent at a young age. A lot of professionals at that time tacitly agreed with this approach; they thought it was just too confusing for the children to go back and forth and to have two fathers. Some even advised fathers that it would be better for the children if they stayed away altogether.

Years of talking with these children and hearing of their struggles as adults with their sense of abandonment by their fathers have taught us that this thinking was wrong. Children, most often very resilient, can adjust well to divorce and visitation. It is the adults who have a more difficult time. For the most part, when adults stop visitation it is for their own selfish reasons.

To custodial parents, who feel as if they carry all the parenting responsibilities, visitation looks remarkably easy. Noncustodial parents have a different perspective. They are the ones who usually do all of the driving, picking their kids up and dropping them off. For almost two weeks at a time they have no children around and lead an "adult" life; then for three days their homes are invaded. Such parents sometimes feel that visitation interferes with their "real" life.

The children usually have fewer toys and things to entertain them at the noncustodial parent's home and, unless the two parents live very close together, the children are cut off from their friends when they go to visit. If they are not in frequent phone contact with the children between visits, noncustodial parents often lose touch with what's going on in the day-to-day lives of their kids. Thus, the combination of fewer toys and no friends puts a lot of pressure on noncustodial parents to entertain in a situation where they are not well tuned in to what's going on with their kids. Unfortunately, the result of all of this is a tendency for noncustodial parents to pull back as the postdecree years go by. Excuses for missing weekends because of business and social activities may become more frequent. As this happens and more time goes by between visits, the situation is compounded and it is that much more difficult to maintain the relationship.

Loving relationships need to be nurtured, even relationships between parents and children. Given the nature of childhood and adolescence, the parent is going to have to take more than half the responsibility for keeping the closeness. If that effort isn't made, if visitation dwindles, the closeness will not be maintained.

Custodial parents will stop, or try to stop, visitation for a myriad of reasons. The single most common reason is failure to recognize the importance of a two-parent relationship for the growth and development of the children. As the postdivorce years go by, the custodial parent and children become more and more of a family, often a stepparent is added, and the weekend visitations sometimes are perceived as an inconvenience or a nuisance. All custodial parents need are a few comments from their children indicating that visitation wasn't wonderful—"All we did was watch TV" or "It was boring"—to consciously or unconsciously start interfering with the process. Too many activities (see previous chapter), family outings, and other events get scheduled, and visitation takes an ever-decreasing priority in the scheme of things.

Sometimes custodial parents try to interfere with visitation because of leftover bitterness from the marriage and divorce. They don't like the ex-spouse and on the basis of this dislike don't think their children should be involved with the parent. This is a terrible injustice to the children. Your ex-spouse may have been terrible, even abusive, to you, but that does not mean that he or she will inevitably be abusive to the children. For someone who has personal reasons for negative feelings about that parent this is a hard call to make. Objectivity simply isn't there. Clearly a parent who is an addict or alcoholic or who is physically, sexually, or emotionally abusive is not someone with whom the children should be spending a lot of time. However, if the children want to continue visiting and the other parent wants visitation to continue, you look like a villain if you attempt to interfere. The best course of action is to work through your attorney or the court. If mediation is available to you, it is the best solution. If not, pursue your legal options. But remember, you cannot arbitrarily make a decision that visitation is not good for your child. You will ruin any cooperative relationship you might have with your ex-spouse, and you run the risk of alienating your child.

Finally, never use the threat of discontinuing visitation as a bargaining chip to get something else from your ex-spouse (e.g., child support, possessions, etc.). Visitation is part of a court-approved legal agreement. If you interfere with it, even if the visiting parent isn't paying child support, you run the risk of being admonished by the court, or worse, held in contempt, and you may well alienate your child.

Children Stopping Visitation

There are a number of reasons why children stop visitation. By far the most frequent reason is their identification with an angry custodial parent (see "Child-Parent Put-downs" in Chapter 3 and "Blame for the Divorce" in Chapter 2). When parents are openly critical of the ex-spouse it practically forces the children to take sides. The side they take is most often that of the parent with whom they live; to do otherwise is to draw battle lines in the home they live in. As the children themselves begin getting angry with the noncustodial parent, they can no longer justify visitation. Excuses for not going are made more and more frequently until eventually visitation stops altogether. In the same vein, children are likely to stop visitation if the noncustodial parent is often critical of the custodial parent. The children won't want to place themselves in this situation on a continual basis, and therefore they stop visiting.

Open deprecation of an ex-spouse in front of the children never serves any useful purpose. It is always detrimental to all of the intrafamily relationships. Yet it is one of the most common problems that children of divorce face today.

Another common reason children stop visitation is that they are bored when they visit. They go to the noncustodial parent's home and do nothing but watch TV. Most often the parent lives sufficiently far from the custodial home to make visiting with friends difficult. There are few toys and the parent makes no provisions to fill the weekends.

In situations where children actually stop visiting, noncustodial parents usually work for part of the visit or are gone for other reasons, and in the evenings they often have social plans, leaving the children alone or with a sitter. They fulfill their obligation to have their children visit but do nothing with them, expecting the children to entertain themselves without the tools (friends and toys) they have at home. So the visits are without much value for the children. Excuses are made, visits are missed, and as the scenario continues, visits become less and less frequent and finally stop altogether.

Keeping visitation interesting is not difficult, but it does require giving of yourself. Playing board games, going to parks, sledding, playing catch, and going to museums, the zoo, local sporting events, or the movies are just some of the activities that will fill a weekend and promote togetherness for children and parent. With a little imagination you will come up with other ideas on your own.

Among other common reasons children stop visitation are stepparents and stepsiblings. When children visiting a parent feel like outsiders because of the attitudes of the stepsiblings and stepparent it can be very difficult (see sections on stepsiblings and stepparents in Chapter 3). Also, children resent visiting a parent only to be baby-sat by the stepparent (regardless of how much they may like him or her) while their mother or father is off attending to other things.

These are the most common reasons children cut back and eventually stop visitation. Some distinction should be made between alterations in visitation made for these reasons and alterations made because the children's growth and developmental needs dictate flexibility (see "Flexibility in Visitation," Chapter 3, and "Changing Needs of Children," this chapter).

Perhaps you wonder why the alcoholism or abusiveness of a parent aren't among the common reasons children stop visitation. If you look at the reasons presented above, they all have a common theme—the disruption in the communication process and hence in the intimate relationship between parent and child. Children will stop visiting abusive parents if in addition to the abuse there is a disruption of the close child-parent attachment. On the other hand, many children will suffer abuse or neglect but still experience attachment. If this happens they will continue to visit unless the custodial parent intervenes.

Authority versus Rigidity in Parenting

Single parenting, either as a custodial or noncustodial parent, is different from parenting in an intact family. As part of the normal development process, children are constantly testing limits. It's actually a healthy reaction; they want to do more, and with doing more, they will learn, comes responsibility. However, single parents often feel their control over their lives is diminished, and it is common for them to try to exercise more control over their children. In an intact family there is another adult with whom to check out ideas on punishment, freedom, and responsibility for the kids. An overly strict parent is usually balanced by a parent who is more lenient.

Check out your parenting ideas. Don't just talk to people who believe the same things you do. Find some balance. Take a P.E.T. (Parent Effectiveness Training) course or other parent training course and find a single parent support group. No one has all the answers, and fresh ideas combined with your own intuition will make you a more competent parent.

Keep in mind that your children's respect is not developed by the imposition of rigid rules or by parental dominance and control. Respect and the following of parental restrictions generally develop in response to a loving authority, one that is tempered with explanations, exceptions, flexibility, compassion, and understanding. I suggest to parents that they think of the rules in their house as two circles, one inside the other. The inner circle consists of a set of rules you don't want the children to disobey but that you expect them to test and occasionally break as they grow. The consequences for these violations are not severe and often consist of nothing more than a conversation between parent and child about why the rule exists. The outer circle represents rules that must not be broken, rules for which consequences of violation are significant. These two circles and the space in between provide room for child-parent discussion and room for growth and some self-determination on the part of the child. The parent, however, retains ultimate control and authority.

Love and devotion do not grow out of rigid control. Furthermore, inflexible control often stifles development. Children will have long-lasting and more deeply involved relationships with parents when their respect comes from authority and love than they will when the respect is born of fear.

Parents Changing Custody

Changing custody from one parent to another is relatively easy as long as this change is wanted and accepted by everyone concerned—both parents and the child or children involved. Changing custody when everyone is not in agreement is extremely difficult and has far-reaching ramifications for all.

Many parents change custody as the years go by because they recognize the changing needs in their children and circumstances in their own lives have shifted. Many of these couples have had cooperative postdivorce years, visitation has been frequent and enjoyed, and with the change, the former custodial parent is guaranteed liberal visitation. Some couples don't even bother with attorneys. The children simply move from one house to the other and child support either stops or reverses. While this is not recommended—attorneys should be used so that both adults can sign an agreed order for everyone's protection—such a process is indicative of the cooperative nature of the relationship. It is in an atmosphere like this that children of divorce can thrive.

Most states have laws that govern change of custody, and if both parents don't agree on the change, then these laws dictate if and how the change occurs. For example, in Illinois, a parent can't modify a judgment on custody within the first two years unless the court rules otherwise, (1) on the basis of an affidavit that demonstrates that the present environment may seriously endanger the child's physical, mental, moral, or emotional health, (2) by clear and convincing evidence that there has been a change in the circumstances of the child or his custodian, and (3) because it finds that the modification of custody is in the best interests of the child.

Two years after any custodial judgment, the requirements for changing custody are less stringent: An affidavit is no longer necessary, and it is no longer required that the children's environment be endangering them physically, mentally, morally, or emotionally. The specifications of items 2 and 3 above remain in effect.[1] You should check with your attorney to find out about the laws that govern changing custody in your state.

Obviously everyone is better off if a change can be agreed on before petitions are filed in court and a legal battle begins. If mediation is available, it is recommended. It increases the possibility that the adults will reach an agreement, and in any event they benefit from a neutral professional's opinion on what is in the best interests of the children.

The most common reasons that parents will seek change in custody are

1. the children are asking for a change (see next section)
2. the custodial parent is endangering the children by his or her alcohol or drug abuse
3. the custodial parent is endangering the children because of a mental condition that has rendered him or her incompetent
4. a belief that sexual and/or physical abuse is taking place in the custodial home
5. the custodial parent is unable to control a misbehaving child
6. the custodial family is moving to another city or state

Remember, children should not be asked which parent they want to live with, or even if they want to change (which is the

[1]Taken from Section 610 of the Illinois Marriage and Dissolution of Marriage Act.

same thing). However, without the support of the children it will
be difficult to get custody changed. Make sure that you are
honestly acting in your children's best interests and not out of
bitterness and vindictiveness toward your ex-spouse. If your motives are not sincere, you could be doing irreparable damage to
several relationships. Also remember that just because a custodial
parent is abusive or becomes emotionally disturbed doesn't mean
that the alternative is better. The child's attachment to that parent, to other people in the home, and to the school and community
all need to be considered in making a custodial change. Because
these are never simple decisions and there are no simple answers,
if both parents do not agree, mediation and other professional help
is clearly indicated.

Children Changing Custody

Throughout this book I have repeated the admonition about
asking children with which parent they want to live. The reason
for not forcing children to divide their loyalty has been explained,
as well as the consequences for putting children in that position.
For the most part, children will avoid such situations. Consequently, when children tell us, after living in the care of one parent, that they now want to live with the other, we listen.

Often custodial parents feel that a child wants to move in with
the other parent because it is much more fun there—fewer responsibilities, restaurants or shows, and, if the money is available, fun
trips. The truth is that children generally want a change in custody to get away from something rather than to go to something.
If children are happy in the custodial home and are bonded and
attached to the people who live there, their loyalties will remain
with the custodial family. If a child really is drawn to the other
parent against the background of a decent custodial home, what
most likely will happen is that the child will ask for increased
visitation, not custodial change.

When children do want a change in custody they will usually
verbalize the desire in positive terms, despite wanting to leave
because of something negative in the custodial home. Unless the

negative is obvious and painful, they will, out of concern for the custodial parent's feelings, usually express the desire to leave with statements like "I've lived with you for five years; it's only fair I live with mom now," or "I'm a boy so I need to be with my dad more."

Children will almost always talk with the noncustodial parent first before saying anything to the custodial parent, in order to check out the noncustodial parent's attitude before burning bridges behind them. Unless there is an urgent need to change, I caution noncustodial parents to move slowly. If children are reporting child abuse or another situation in which they are in some danger, then quick action is warranted. Otherwise a more deliberate approach is indicated.

The first statements a child makes to the noncustodial parent may be something along the line of "You know, sometimes I think about what it would be like if I lived here all the time," or, near the end of the visitation or vacation, "I hate having to go home." Comments like these are feelers. The child is fishing for an accepting response. Such feelings don't automatically mean, however, that the child wants to move. Don't be overanxious and force the issue. A simple "I'm disappointed too when you leave, so I'll look forward to your next visit," conveys love and acceptance to the child.

It may be months after the first feelers before a child says he or she wants to move in. The noncustodial parent will be told first. As a noncustodial parent you have the responsibility to your child, yourself, and your former spouse to proceed cautiously. The child needs to talk to the custodial parent, and the other parent should encourage this and not move legally until it is done. This process ensures that (1) this is really what the child wants, (2) the problem in the custodial home can't be resolved, and (3) both parents aren't involved in child-parent put-downs and the child isn't pitting the parents against each other (see relevant sections in Chapter 3). A distinction needs to be made between a child's sincere need and desire for change of custody and a child's anger over, for example, parental discipline. The slow, thoughtful, and deliberate approach advocated here will help everyone involved to determine whether or not a change of custody is the right decision.

Children under the age of nine are not likely to ask for a change of custody. If there are serious problems in the custodial home, they will probably just complain. They are too young and hence too insecure to ask for a change. Children of high school age who are well connected to a peer group are also less likely to change. They will also complain, but in addition will absent themselves from home, spending large amounts of time with friends and at part-time jobs. Most requests for custodial change come from children ages nine through fourteen.

The most common reasons that children will seek a change in custody are

1. unavailability of the custodial parent *both* physically and emotionally—children can tolerate the physical absence as long as they feel emotionally connected
2. extremely strict and rigid parenting practices, e.g., constant use of the child as maid and/or babysitter, long periods of "grounding" as punishment, removal of phone privileges, friends not allowed in the home
3. excessive corporal punishment
4. stepparent a child doesn't get along with, especially if it is the stepparent who is responsible for 2 or 3 above
5. physical or sexual abuse in the custodial home
6. stepbrothers or sisters or natural siblings with whom a child can't get along

Remember that children will most likely leave something unacceptable to go to something that appears better. Both sides of the equation must be in effect for a child to ask for a change. For example, a child won't leave an unavailable custodial parent for an unavailable noncustodial parent, but that child might leave a parent who is unavailable for a parent who is remarried if the child likes and gets along with the stepparent and there is a sense of family in that home.

Children's Guilt

In divorce, children are always polarized, even when their parents are not angry and treat each other well. The very nature of divorce—parents who used to be together going in different directions—forces this polarization. Once custody and visitation are established, any change in the system at the request of the child is likely to produce guilt, because the child is pulling away from one side and toward the other. Regardless of the justification for such change, a child will understand, on some level, that one parent is experiencing pain as a result. Guilt, if severe enough, can lead to lowered self-esteem and depression, with concomitant withdrawal and poor performance in school.

The only way for this guilt to be moderated and perhaps eliminated is for the parent who has suffered from the change to honestly and openly support it. If the child feels his or her actions have not hurt a parent, the guilt will be minimized. Therefore, I strongly urge parents to support custody or visitation changes that are in the child's best interests. This is obviously easier when there is an increase or decrease in visitation than when there is a change in custody.

When custody is changed, I almost always recommend that the child, and frequently the child and the new custodians, go through a brief period of professional counseling. The therapy will help the child work through his or her guilt and the family therapy will help the new custodial family deal more effectively with the change.

Chapter 5

Conclusions and Tests

Future Custody Trends

Nowhere in the broad field of child and adolescent development has there been as much change and has knowledge advanced as much as in the area of custody and visitation. As recently as two decades ago, custody almost always was granted to the mother, and fathers would either just visit or perhaps disappear altogether, abandoning their parental obligations and their children as well. Today fathers have become more and more active as noncustodial parents, in joint parenting agreements, and as custodial parents. This continuing trend is a sociological as well as a legal one. As women have demanded equal rights in areas they had been neglected in, the trend has influenced men to equalize areas of their own. Clearly custody is one of these areas. In addition, the legal system has taken meaningful steps to insure that noncustodial fathers exercise their financial responsibilities. Forcing them to pay child support has helped keep many fathers involved with children they otherwise might have abandoned.

Now the mental health and counseling professions have begun to catch up with these trends, helping to advance them further, and at the same time enabling the various family members to adjust better to the trauma of divorce. Groups for children of divorce are now common in schools and churches throughout the country. Groups for single parents have also become widely established. These types of support groups are excellent vehicles for children and adults struggling with postdivorce trauma. Psychologists and social workers have also grown in sophistication during the last two decades and are better prepared to cope with and treat the more devastating effects of divorce.

Finally, the advent of mediation for custody and visitation disputes has effectively reduced the amount of litigated conflict in this area. Where mediation is court ordered and the mediators are used as expert witnesses, litigation is reduced even further. In DuPage County, the second largest county in Illinois (an area of suburban communities outside of Chicago), over 500 cases came to the court in two years involving either divorce or postdecree disputes over custody and visitation. All 500 cases were ordered to mediation, and only 5 percent of them were actually litigated in the courts. The remainder ended with the parties either agreeing in mediation or accepting the mediator's recommendations for custody and visitation. Mediation has resulted in a much faster and more amicable divorce process and obviously a better adjustment for the children. In the years to come we will see more involvement of mediation in the divorce process. Our early experience with it has demonstrated that the marriage of the mental health professions and the legal system is in the best interests of the children. It has shortened the divorce process where custody is at issue; it has helped minimize the adversarial nature of divorce; and it has acted as an early intervention program, spotting troubled adults and children earlier than otherwise would have occurred.

As might be expected, the trends in custody also indicate that more men are getting involved as custodial parents. In the sample cited above, 22 percent of the mediated cases resulted in men receiving full custody, joint custody with physical possession of the children, or joint physical custody. Figures on paternal custody are not available for divorce cases that are agreed on without mediation or litigation. However, if the male custody rate as determined by mediation is any reflection of what is happening generally, then paternal custody is clearly on the rise.

Who is the best parent, regardless of gender, is the question that courts, mental health professionals, and parents are striving to answer. With that concern in mind, the following test has been developed. It is hoped that an honest completion of this test by divorcing couples will help them assess their parental roles and, in turn, facilitate a custodial decision without bitter litigation.

Shapiro Custody Determination Test

The Shapiro Custody Determination Test (SCDT) has been developed on the basis of my fifteen years of work as a clinical psychologist conducting custody evaluations and doing conciliation and mediation work with divorcing and divorced couples. Many of the questions asked in the SCDT are asked during typical mediation sessions. In honestly answering these questions, you and your spouse will begin to recognize the different levels of attachment that your child has to both of you. In the majority of family situations, it will become clear with whom the child should reside once this test is completed. Where it is not clear, mediation, if available, or professional help is recommended. This test should not be used as the only determination of custody. It is meant to be used as a guide. The test should be used in conjunction with other sections of the book (e.g., Chapter 2, "Custody of Infants and Preschoolers" and "Should the Children Be Split Up?"). Directions for taking the SCDT follow, and directions for scoring it are at the end of the test.

Whether or not you use the SCDT to help in resolving the custody question, completion of the test will force you to appraise your child-rearing practices and the interactions that indicate the level of attachment between you and your child.

Directions

Each adult should answer the test questions independently. The answers to the questions should apply to the last year to year and a half. Answer each question by putting either an M (for mother) or an F (for father) in the space provided. If you feel that both of you are equal on any particular question, put both M and F in the answer space. If a question does not apply, leave it blank.

Do not be concerned with how many M's or F's you are writing in. The questions are weighted, and the actual number of M's or F's alone does not make up the test score.

SCDT

1. Which parent is more supportive of education? _____
2. Which parent is most encouraging of socializing? _____
3. Which parent is most influential in teaching manners (table manners, respect for adults, etc.)? _____
4. Which parent is more responsible for teaching homemaking skills (cooking, cleaning, care for clothes, etc.)? _____
5. Which parent is more responsible for teaching home maintenance skills (lawn care, painting, fix-it, etc.)? _____
6. Which parent is more effective as a reliable source of information on life (e.g., sex, love, death, religion)? _____
7. Which parent is most supportive of religious education? _____
8. Which parent is more responsible for taking the child to the doctor? _____
9. Which parent is more likely to watch television with the child? _____
10. Which parent is most responsible for hygiene (bathing, brushing teeth, hair, haircuts, deodorant, etc.)? _____
11. Who is the parent regularly in the home that sends the children off to school? _____
12. Who is the parent more regularly in the house when the child comes home from school (or the first parent home after the child comes home)? _____
13. Which parent knows the names of three of the child's friends (other than relatives)? _____
14. Which parent most often gets up in the middle of the night with a sick child? _____
15. Who is the parent most likely to attend school conferences, school open houses, etc.? _____

16. Which parent is most supportive of having the children's friends in the house? _____
17. Which parent is more positive in their orientation toward life (optimistic, confident, upbeat, happy)? _____
18. Which parent is the same sex as the child? _____
19. Which parent is more likely to keep promises? _____
20. Which parent is most supportive of extracurricular activities (music lessons, scouting, sports, etc.)? _____
21. Which parent is most active with extracurricular activities (attends games, drives to lessons, etc.)? _____
22. Which parent is more likely to initiate family activities (going to the zoo, going to a ball game, going to grandma's, etc.)? _____
23. Which parent has the extended family the child is most involved with (grandparents, aunts, uncles, cousins)? _____
24. Which parent is more physically available to the child? _____
25. Which parent is better in an emergency? _____
26. Which parent is a more evenhanded and reliable disciplinarian? _____
27. Which parent is better at comforting and reassuring in difficult situations? _____
28. Which parent is more patient and effective in dealing with sibling problems? _____
29. Who is the child more likely to turn to with a problem? _____
30. Who does the child go to most comfortably about everyday things (school, friends, feelings?) _____
31. Which parent is a better and more patient listener? _____
32. Which parent spends more time interacting with the child? _____
33. Which parent communicates more clearly with the child? _____
34. Which parent communicates the most with the child? _____
35. Which parent demonstrates love more clearly to the child (through words and actions—touching, hugging, etc.)? _____

36. Who is the parent most available to help the child
     with homework?   _____

37. Who is the parent most involved in talking with the
     child about friends and problems with friends?   _____

38. Which parent is more likely to play inside games with
     the child?   _____

39. Which parent is more likely to play outside games
     with the child?   _____

40. Which parent does a child say he or she wants to live
     with?   _____

41. With which parent will the other children reside?   _____

Scoring

Scoring the SCDT is easy. Questions 1 through 9 are worth 2
points each. Questions 10 through 28 are each worth 3 points.
Questions 29 through 41 are worth 5 points apiece. If any of your
answers have both M and F, then divide the points for that question equally (for example, if question 35 has an M,F answer, M
gets 2½ points and F receives 2½ points). If a question does not
apply, no points are assigned. There are 140 total possible points.
In a family where both mother and father are active participants
in child-rearing, their scores will each range between 50 and 90
points. If both scores are between 50 and 90 I recommend getting
professional help in deciding the custody issue. If the scores are
outside the 50 to 90 point range, then the parent who scored
higher than 90 points should strongly be considered for custody.
A parent whose score is less than 50 is not nearly as involved as
the other parent in day-to-day child-rearing activities and not
likely to be closely bonded; this parent would fit in better as a
noncustodial parent in the child's life. If both you and your spouse
take the test independently there should be no more than a 10
percent variance between your scores for yourself and your spouse
and your spouse's scores for you and him- or herself. For example,
if your score for yourself is 60 and your score for your spouse is
80, then your spouse's score for you should be between 54 and 66
while his or her score should be between 72 and 88. If there is

greater than 10 percent variance between your scores for yourself and your spouse and his or her scores, then both of you see yourselves differently enough in relationship to your children to warrant professional help with your decision.

Divorce Destructiveness Scale

We all assume that divorce itself—the splitting of a family—is what is destructive to children. Indeed it is; however, children are very resilient and will survive divorce if parents protect them from their own bitterness and anger and do not selfishly use their children as pawns in the divorce process. Furthermore, as parents we often get lost in the day-to-day struggle to cope with our new lives. Jobs, finances, friends, arrangements for the kids, and the daily routines of shopping, cleaning, and preparing meals all demand our attention. Existing becomes a priority, and for a while, some of the more subtle nuances of our lives and the lives of our children may go unnoticed. As long as our children appear to be coping, we often aren't aware of the pain and the emotional trauma that lingers beneath the surface. The following series of questions has been designed to assist parents in understanding the destructive potential that divorce has on children. They will also help you refocus your attention on the emotional well-being of the children. To see how you are doing or how you've done, and to see how your child is doing, answer the following questions.

Divorce Destructiveness Scale

	YES	NO
1. Did you and your spouse separate between two weeks and two months after telling the children about the divorce?	_____	_____
2. Did you and your spouse together tell the children about the divorce?	_____	_____

3. Were you able to tell your children about the divorce without blaming each other? _____ _____

4. Have you been able to avoid blaming each other in front of the children since telling them about the divorce? _____ _____

5. Did you fight over custody? _____ _____

6. Did you avoid asking your children to make choices about which parent to live with? _____ _____

7. Were you able to avoid having the children change schools? _____ _____

8. Were the children able to stay in the same home following the divorce? _____ _____

9. Does the noncustodial parent live within a half-hour's drive from the custodial home? _____ _____

10. Does the noncustodial parent see the children on at least 15 percent of the days of a month? _____ _____

11. Do the noncustodial parent and children talk on the phone between visits? _____ _____

12. Does the noncustodial parent do more than babysit during visitation (play games, help with homework, go places, etc.)? _____ _____

13. Is the custodial parent supportive of visitation? _____ _____

14. Is the custodial parent supportive of the other parent? _____ _____

15. Is the noncustodial parent supportive of the custodial parent? _____ _____

16. Do both parents (and stepparents) avoid parent-parent put-downs? _____ _____

17. Do both parents (and stepparents) avoid the traps of child-parent put-downs? _____ _____

18. Is there flexibility in visitation? _____ _____

19. Were all the children kept together after the divorce? _____ _____

20. Is the custodial parent competent? _____ _____

21. Is the other parent competent? _____ _____

22. Is the custodial parent desirable? _____ _____

23. Is the other parent desirable? _____ _____

24. Do both parents avoid discussing the settlement (i.e., money) with the children? _____ _____
25. Do both parents help the children get gifts for the other parent? _____ _____
26. Are both parents supportive of the gift giving to the children by the other parent? _____ _____
27. Do the parents communicate with each other around health and education issues of their children? _____ _____
28. Are you supportive and understanding of your children's reactions to visitation? _____ _____
29. Do you enjoy the time spent with your children? _____ _____
30. Do you enjoy the time spent away from your children? _____ _____
31. Are your children involved in some after-school activities? _____ _____
32. Are their extracurricular activities coordinated with visitation? _____ _____
33. Does the custodial parent attend more than half of the children's after-school activities? _____ _____
34. Does the other parent frequently attend after-school activities? _____ _____
35. Does the child look forward to visitation? _____ _____
36. Does the child enjoy returning to the custodial home? _____ _____
37. Has there been maintenance or improvement in the children's grades pre- and postdivorce? _____ _____
38. Has there been maintenance or improvement in the children's moods pre- and postdivorce? _____ _____
39. Has there been maintenance or improvement in the children's weight (besides normal growth) pre- and postdivorce? _____ _____
40. Has there been maintenance or improvement in the children's sleeping patterns pre- and postdivorce? _____ _____

41. Has there been maintenance or improvement
    in the children's level of social activities
    pre- and postdivorce?   _____ _____
42. Do the children get along well with
    stepparents?   _____ _____
43. Do the children get along with stepbrothers
    and stepsisters?   _____ _____
44. Have both parents refrained from arguing in
    front of the children postdivorce?   _____ _____
45. Do the children feel their parents get along
    okay since the divorce?   _____ _____

Using the Divorce Destructiveness Scale

If you have answered all the above questions affirmatively,
then you have provided an ideal situation for your child to survive
divorce. Because none of us is perfect, most parents answering the
Divorce Destructiveness Scale will have several "no's" in their
responses. This is to be expected. However, if there are more than
seven no's among your responses, or if some of the key questions
(e.g., questions 10, 13, 15, 16, 37, 38, 39, and 42) are answered no,
then it is very likely your child is not adjusting well to your divorce. Every child is different, and each divorce has its own
unique characteristics. It is difficult to predict the destructive
potential without knowing all the factors involved. The purpose
of this scale has been to highlight potential difficulties. If in doing
so you have become concerned about the adjustment of your child,
then evaluation by a psychologist or other trained mental health
professional who has experience in working with children of divorce is recommended.

Some Comments: Making the Next Marriage Work

Why a section on marriage in a divorce book? And why make
it the concluding section? The majority of people who get divorced
will remarry, and the majority of those who remarry will do so in

the first five years following their divorce. Making the next marriage work is vitally important to them and almost as important to their children.

The vast majority of people divorcing today were born in the late 40s, the 50s, and the 60s; they are the post-World War II generation. The members of this "me-first" generation, as it has been called, are more demanding of need gratification and less capable of coping with frustration than were their parents. They were raised in a more permissive environment with less responsibility, and they were given more than were their predecessors. They have made more money and traveled more extensively than their parents. During their development they have been exposed more to representations of romance and passion (previously a private learning experience) by movies, literature, and television than any other generation.

The combination of raised expectations and less ability to cope with frustration has resulted in couples giving up on marital situations that could have been salvaged with greater determination and resolve, work and compromise.

As you enter your next loving relationship, the chances of making it work are better because you are older, more mature, and wiser from the experience of your first marriage. Recognize and remember this time that the heat and passion of the union will not remain at its initial intensity; that the all-encompassing preoccupation of your love will soon be interfered with by the day-to-day realities of kids, finances, jobs, and extended family.

Your spouse should be your best friend, and your marriage an intimate relationship in which the two of you are deeply committed in a mutually giving, affectionate, and loving bond. It is based on both of you wanting a love relationship and wanting to give unselfishly to your partner. It has a sense of commitment and trust. In the sharing, both emotional and sexual, grows the feeling of specialness that is the essence of marriage.

In addition to your maturity, the biggest difference between your first marriage and the second is the children. Their adjustment to divorce, custody and visitation arrangements, remarriage, new schools, and friends will place immediate strain on the new marriage. In order to survive, you both will need a unity of purpose that has at its core a concern for the emotional and moral growth and development of the children. It may mean fewer moments of quiet adult time. It will mean a concentration on the needs of the children, now greater because of what they've been through. Your ability to cope with frustration will be challenged. Your first priority in this marriage must be the children. If it is not, then their problems will be such that it will be difficult for you and your spouse to enjoy your relationship. However, if you attend to their needs, it will make the time the two of you have far more enjoyable. Remember also that the length of the custody time—a few years or perhaps a decade—is short when compared to an entire lifespan.

As you enter your next relationship, the possibility of making it work will be challenged by ex-spouses, children, and blended families and a multitude of family and friends still caught up in the bitterness and disappointments of the old marriage and divorce. If all of this is understood, the heat and passion will turn into a warm glow, and you will both work at and compromise in your marriage to maintain the trust and exclusive specialness that are at the foundation of your union.